FOOTPRINTS IN THE MUD OF TIME

The Alternative Story of York

RESEARCHED & WRITTEN
BY GRAHAM RHODES

FOOTPRINTS IN THE MUD OF TIME
THE ALTERNATIVE STORY OF YORK

FIRST PUBLISHED 1998 BY CILIBUGA PUBLISHING
AN IMPRINT OF TEMPLAR PUBLISHING, TOCKWITH

ISBN Number 0.9521015.2.1

PRINTED BY
QUACKS THE PRINTERS
GRAPE LANE, YORK

FOOTPRINTS IN THE MUD OF TIME
THE ALTERNATIVE STORY OF YORK

RESEARCHED & WRITTEN BY GRAHAM RHODES

Lives of great men all remind us
We can make our lives sublime
And, departing, leave behind us
Footsteps on the sands of time.
LONGFELLOW

FOREWORD

By The Right Honourable Hugh Bayley - M.P. for York.

"I hope you enjoy this light hearted look at York's history as much as I did. Personally I like the invading Celts who lost their blue woad in the cut-price Roman swimming baths.......
but you will have to choose your own favorite events from this informative but not-too-serious cavort through the story of our beautiful and historic city. I wonder what vole pie was like?"

Hugh Bayley M.P. The House of Commons.
29 Jan 1998.

INTRODUCTION

Some people, especially historians, take history far too seriously. I first had that thought as a board rubber bounced off my head during a history lesson at my old school.

Having written the scripts for such programmes as "The Tale of Beatrix Potter", "Roman Colchester", "The History of Liverpool Ship Building", and "The York Story", I have read book after book of history and have discovered that there is very little that is new. All they contain are a few basic facts, and everything else is just the writer's personal interpretation and theories. So I thought I'd throw my hat in the ring with all the others. In consequence this book is my interpretation of the history of the City of York. It doesn't really matter if some of the contents are spurious, fictitious or downright lies, it's meant to be something that seems alien among the academics and stentorian historians, it's meant to be fun. It's meant to be as much fun and as historically accurate as a ride in a time car along a reproduction Viking village. As much fun and as historically accurate as getting drunk in a genuine Irish Theme Pub during York's annual Viking Festival.

The book would have been impossible without the help of Michael Sessions & Quacks the Printers, Mr & Mrs Nattrass and Angela Knox who did the proof reading, and Lynda Greenwood, my solicitor who is standing by! It is dedicated with much affection to the people and the City Of York and to anyone who has bought it, who in doing so has helped me pay the bills that have mounted up in the time it's taken to write it. Finally and more importantly, it's for anyone who ever thought that history was boring, and especially to any other kids whose teachers think that a board rubber bouncing off a young head is still a valid teaching aid.

Graham Rhodes - York 1998.

CHAPTER ONE

EBORACUM - ROMAN YORK.

By AD 47 the Roman Empire controlled a section of Britain that stretched in an imaginary line from the River Humber to the River Severn controlled by fortresses established at Lincoln and Gloucester. Above that line, controlling an area from the Trent to the Cheviot Hills, was a Celtic tribe called the *Brigantes.* The Romans had made an alliance with their Queen *Cartimandua,* who by all accounts was something of a hellion. She took to the Roman way of life like a duck takes to water and, in the tradition of all Roman rulers, was soon having numerous lovers and affairs, playing the fiddle and watching buildings burn.

This new behaviour annoyed her husband *Venutius*, who had been quite happy with the way things were, and, in AD 69, the they fell out in a big way. One day when she was out visiting her Roman paramour, *Venutius* built himself a new fort near Richmond, and threw her out of the kingdom locking the door behind her. The resulting rumpus was heard throughout the Roman Empire.

Meanwhile, back in Rome there had been a number of job rationalisations, restructures and reshuffles which led to the death of four Emperors in the same year. *Vespasian*, who had once been a commander in Britain, took over the job and set about establishing himself as Emperor. In a short space of time he put down rebellions in Judea and on the Rhine, and he needed the news of *Cartimandua's* rebellion like he needed a hole in the head. He appointed a friend of his, one *Quintus Petilius Cerialis,* as Governor of Britain and sent him off on the next boat to sort things out. *Cerialis* sailed from Holland and established his forces at Lincoln, and in AD 71 they marched out from their base, hacking and slashing their way up the A15 until they reached the A19 and marched straight on, into the tribal lands of the Celtic Brigantes.

Eventually this force came to an area of land guarded by two rivers, the Ouse and Foss, known by the Brigantes as *Eboracum.* In Celtic this name meant either "a place where the yew trees grow" or, "that cucumber allotment owned by a bloke called Ebor". On seeing the grove of yew trees and the cooling river, *Quintus Petilius Ceralis* decided it would be a good place to take a rest.

As the legionnaires bathed their aching feet in the river the commander looked around and decided that he had walked far enough. After his rest he called a stop to all the marching, hacking and slashing and ordered a large wooden fort from a local Celtic builder called *Portafortia,* based at nearby Huntington.

Once the fort was erected the Romans settled in, changed its name to *Eboracum,* and began the unenviable task of bringing civilization to the wild Yorkshire folk. To this day it is debatable whether or not they succeeded. They introduced many innovations such as aqueducts and wine, which were good things, and laws and taxes, which were very bad things. They also introduced the Roman Baths, which were very wet things.

The baths were not just for enjoyment. They were in fact a sneaky way of subduing the war-like Celts. When the Romans noticed a large army of blue painted tribal warriors waiting outside the gates of *Eboracum* they opened their baths to the general public, and quickly organised a special early morning rate for local tribes. This puzzled the Celts who had never seen a swimming pool before, and they soon joined the queue. Despite the Celts not having brought their swimming trunks the Romans allowed them entry and left the Celts splashing happily away.

After some time in the pool the Celts suddenly noticed that all their blue woad had been washed away. With great terror the tribal warriors realised two things. First, that without their paint they no longer looked fierce, and secondly they were now stark bollock naked. Shamed at their sudden nudity the Celts quickly left the pool and tried to sneak out of the fortress, but an alert Roman Guard spotted them and, alerted by the sound of his laughter, the rest of the guard came running.

Afraid of the slings and arrows of outrageous Roman laughter the Celts fled through the fortress gates, never to return. It is believed that this event is the origin of the well known saying "It'll all come out in the wash."

With the Celts subdued, the Romans had nothing much to do and so in AD 108 they set about improving their fortress and began to rebuild it in stone. This came as a relief to many of the Roman Legionnaires who for a number of years had suffered badly from splinters, but for the local inhabitants it was the start of an inconvenient building process that blocked roads and streets, and caused much traffic congestion. A tradition that is still continuing today.

When it was eventually finished *Eboracum* was a walled fortress housing the *Principia,* the military headquarters, along with a number of smiths, shrines, bars, shops and fast food outlets. They also built a wooden bridge across the river Ouse.

This fortress attracted the attention of various local tribes who realised that rather than fight the Romans, it was much more profitable to do business with them. There was a sudden demand for building materials and food, especially bread and meat, and someone had to supply it. Soon all around the fortress walls the local people, eager not to miss out on a good thing, began to build many hovels, butchers shops and small sandwich stalls from which they did a very brisk trade.

In order to make themselves feel more at home, the Roman troops demanded many items that were not available locally. Olive oil and wine were imported all the way from Spain and France in *amphorae,* a type of large pottery jar. However, as there was money back on them, there was a constant shortage of these jars. Discovering it was impossible to store olive oil and wine in anything else the Romans decided to opened up their own pottery and make some *amphorae* of their own. This pottery business was run by a retired legionnaire named *Filus Micupup* and is believed to have been somewhere in the Peasholme Green area of the town. It must have been a very successful venture, as it not only held the catering contract for the entire fortress, but also made a large number of small statues of local gods and an even larger number of pottery mugs with *"A Present From Eboracum"*, emblazoned on their sides.

However it was just after AD 120, when the Ninth Legion left York, that the pottery business really took off big style. The Ninth Legion was replaced by the Sixth, a legion comprising men from the Greek part of the Roman Empire. These excitable new troops brought with them the Greek habit of smashing their plates after every meal, a habit brought about by an appalling lack of washing up liquid in Greece. This state of affairs was noticed by *Filus Micupup,* who encouraged the legionnaires not only to smash their plates, but also their cups, saucers and anything else made of pottery that they could get their hands on. He bought the broken bits back, remade them into more pots and sold them at 100% mark up. The resulting boom in business made *Filus* a very rich man. It is also the reason why so little Roman pottery has ever been dug up in York.

The departure and subsequent disappearance of the Ninth Legion has been the subject of many speculations. Some theories claim they travelled to Lower Germany on a special away-day trip and lost their return tickets. Some claim that they were selected to play in a version of the once popular, pan-European games called "It's A Knock Out" and that they were drawn away against the Parthians where they lost so badly they never bothered to come home. Others claim that they marched north to disappear forever among the mists and heather of Highland Scotland. Some even claim that they never disappeared at all but just got transferred somewhere else and that all the disappearance theories were put together to provide historical pundits and authors a gravy train in the writing of novels and other books.

The Sixth Legion were brought to Britain by the Roman Emperor *Hadrian* who due to the fact that as a kid had once been given a set of Lego bricks for Christmas, was hell bent on building walls. This habit so annoyed the citizens of Rome whose city was built up already and who had no use for further masonry, that the senate sent him off to the furthest part of the Empire where a wall would come in handy. After wandering all around Europe looking for walls to build *Hadrian* ended up in York, but finding the city already had walls, he pushed onto the frontier of the Roman Empire and found a perfect place for one. He built his wall in a line that stretched from Newcastle to Carlisle.

Throughout the following centuries an argument has raged whether the intention of the wall was to prevent the Picts from attacking the Romans, or to prevent the Romans from pushing even deeper north and attacking the Picts. Whatever the reason, the wall marked the northern most boundary of the Roman Empire, until another Lego inspired Roman called *Antonine* turned up on the scene and tried to do one better, further north. (He didn't succeed. It was a very little wall and hardly worth a mention!).

Around AD 200 the Romans rebuilt the city walls of *Eboracum* once again, this time erecting a series of large
entrance gates (which seems a pretty obvious thing to do when you think about it). Again it seems that a local specialist building company was used as their trade mark was used in the naming of these gates, which were *Porta Principalis* (where Bootham Bar now stands), *Porta Principalis Sinistra,* (where Kings Square stands), *Porta Decumana,* (about half way along Lord Mayors Walk), and *Porta Praetoria,* (where St. Helen's Square meets Coney Street and Lendal). They eventually finished rebuilding around AD 208, which was just as well as in the following year *Porta Eboracum* played host to another Roman Emperor, *Septimius Severus,* so called because he was very severe and was born in September.

Severus had decided to pay the city a visit due to the fact that the Picts had discovered how to make ladders and were climbing all over Hadrian's Wall and creeping across to attack the northern most Roman villas. As the visit was deemed official and the Roman Empire was picking up the tab, *Severus* brought his wife and kids along with him, (The Empress *Julia Domna* and his sons *Geta* and *Caracalla*). Not wanting to miss out on a free trip, and claiming that "what was good enough for the Emperor was good enough for them", the rest of the Roman government also came along.

This sudden influx of heavy duty Romans put a great strain on the available accommodation in the city and a number of bed and breakfast establishments were hastily built to house them all. This led to such another round of building and re-building and blocking up of roads that the native people of *Eboracum* soon wished that *Hadrian* was still around as at least, he had the decency to indulge his building fetish miles away from the city.

In AD 211 *Severus,* who had been feeling a bit off for a while, died. However his own death did not come as a surprise to him, unlike the deaths of many unfortunate Picts whom he had been beating the crap out of at the time. Indeed *Severus* believed he had been warned of his imminent departure from the world by experiencing a number of ill omens and bad dreams. One of these ill omens was recorded by a Roman writer called *Dipusmepenin.*

It seems that on one of his regular visits to the Temple of Bellona, *Severus* discovered that the animals prepared for sacrifice were not their usual white colour, they were black. This was considered jolly bad form and so he stamped out of the Temple in a huff and began to walk home when he discovered that he was being followed by a giant black chicken.

No matter how fast he walked, the chicken still followed him. He tried walking through the many alleyways and snickelways in the town. He tried turning corners and running like mad, but every time he turned round there was the chicken still following on behind him. Eventually he reached his lodgings where he collapsed in a heap and promptly died. Eerily, the giant chicken was never seen again. This event was commemorated on a small stone tablet, engraved with the image of a chicken and the feet of Mercury, the Roman God of fast running, which was found during an excavation at Wellington Row in 1988-89.

Severus was succeeded as Emperor of Rome by his son *Caracalla,* who as soon as the funeral was decently over, quickly left the city and returned to Rome. On his arrival in the capital he promptly promoted *Eboracum* to the status of *Colonia,* a regional capital. Why he did this action is uncertain, however some historians believe that it could have been to appease a large number of influential citizens of *Eboracum* who once witnessed him climbing out of a giant chicken costume in a back alley at the rear of his father's lodgings.

Eboracum expanded in the late second century. Streets were rebuilt, new buildings were put up, traffic was congested, and the swimming pool was extended to Olympic length. The town filled with craftsmen, tinkers, traders, more butchers and even more sandwich shops. The riverside docks, based on the River Foss, were expanded. Items such as stone, pottery, jewellery, cloth, corn, coal, lead and gypsum were imported and exported along the river to the Humber and then on to the Continent. Also more exotic goods were imported from all over the Empire. All along the banks of the Ouse crates of peacocks tongues were stacked side by side with crates of sardines, and tins of anchovies. Pizzas arrived by the ship load. The ships also brought some less welcome imports, pasta, black olives, rats and rabbits. The rats brought bubonic plague with them, the rabbits just brought more rabbits.

The many foreign residents and legionnaires living in *Eboracum* brought with them many strange religious cults. As well as cults that worshipped such well known Roman Gods as Diana, (The Goddess of the Hunted, charities and tabloid journalism), Mars (the God of War and chocolate bars), Mithras (a cult based around the Persian Sun God and followed by Roman soldiers), there were also a number of lesser known cults.

During the Wellington Row excavations of 1988, the site of a small temple dedicated the Cult of the Screaming Baboon was uncovered. The followers of this weird cult seem to have worshipped their deity to ensure that they would be relieved of piles, whilst the priests always carried a small jar of healing balm and acted more like stress counsellors than religious leaders. It is believed that inside their small Temple fellow sufferers would gather and offer each other advice on their treatment, whilst sitting on deep feather filled cushions. These remains are only the second of their type to be found in Northern Europe.

Another strange religion was "The Cult of the Small Furry Animal". The followers of this cult were of the belief that certain types of small furry animals represented sexual parts of the human anatomy, and worshipped them accordingly. This underground cult came to an abrupt end around AD 220 when its leader was discovered in bed with three rabbits, two gerbils, a small hen and a large jar of olive oil, and driven out of the town. It is believed that remains of this ancient practice can still be found in the Northern "sport" of plunging ferrets down one's trousers.

The Romans were a very suspicious people and always consulted soothsayers, oracles and fortune tellers before making any major decisions, such as whether or not they should get out of bed that morning. Unlike today's society, where we glance at the horoscope column in the morning paper before getting paranoid about the rest of the day, Roman society was paranoid all the time. They looked for signs and omens everywhere, and, as with all people who go looking for such things, they usually found them. All manner of things and events were deemed lucky or unlucky.

For instance, startling a peacock before the sun had risen on Lupintide Trumpday, was considered the worst possible omen. Anyone unfortunate enough to do such a thing would be struck dead within the hour. If a person fell foul of this omen they would be advised to go home and go straight to bed, as it would save a lot of people a lot of time and trouble finding their body and carrying it back later.

A bee sting was considered as a good omen, especially for the onlookers whom the bee had chosen to ignore. It was also deemed very bad luck if a flock of starlings passed overhead as a Roman was watching badgers mate in a grove of oak trees.

Mind you the Celtic tribes were just as superstitious. Entire tribes would walk around with the paranoid fear of the sky falling on their heads, a custom that originated in Gaul. Originally the Celts had been protected by the power of their Druidic religion, but since the Roman army had rounded up and killed all their Druids at Anglesey, they felt a bit insecure to say the least.

Things got really complicated as more and more Celtic tribes allied themselves with the Romans. Many of the tribesmen would act as guides, horsemen or mercenaries for the Romans. Things came to a head when a joint patrol of Romans and Celts were sent from *Eboracum* to relieve a besieged fortress on the Roman Wall. Being so superstitious before they left to fight, the soldiers and mercenaries had to visit so many different temples, say so many prayers, make so many offerings to different gods, goddesses, furry animals and small round white stones, that by the time they were ready to leave not only was the fortress lost, it had been dismantled and the stones now formed a small visitor centre on the banks of Loch Lomond.

For reasons best known to themselves the Romans believed that it was possible to foretell the future by reading omens from the entrails of animals. This rumour seems to have been put about by the butchers of *Eboracum.* Soon so great was the resulting demand for offal that many of them stopped making offal based meat products like black puddings, sausages, pies and other savories in order to sell entrails directly to the general public.

Even this did not fully meet the supply, and the price of entrails leapt up. Soon only the rich and favoured could use the entrails of the more common animals such as cow, pig and sheep, whilst the poorer people were reduced to attempting to tell their fortunes by examining the entrails of dead hedgehogs, and other small mammals, squashed on the Roman Roads by the many passing chariots and carts.

Towards the end of the third century, *Diocletian* (AD 284-AD 305) became the new Roman Emperor. After taking the job on the man quickly realised that ruling an empire the size of the Roman Empire was not just bloody difficult, it was virtually impossible. As a result he invented a system called Tetrarachy which divided the Empire into two halves, eastern and western. He put two emperors (a senior and a junior) in charge of each half and then subdivided each area into a number of different provinces. Thus Britain became four provinces each with its separate layers of administration and levels of authority.

This was a good idea for *Diocletian* as, when a problem occurred, it had to go through so many levels of bureaucracy and pass through so many different people, that by the time it reached his desk the problem had usually gone away. If it hadn't gone away the problem was usually someone else's fault somewhere down the line, and they would get a jolly good arse kicking from everyone else above them. Instead of having a sign on his desk that read "The buck stops here!" *Diocletain* had a sign that read, "If the buck comes anywhere near this bloody desk, someone, somewhere is going to get their arse kicked!"

This system of holding onto power is the ultimate survival tool for anyone at the top of the heap, and it is interesting to note that many present day institutions such as Banks, Building Societies, G.N.E.R., The Gas Board and National Health Trusts still operate such a system.

Eboracum remained a capital town, although of the much smaller province of *Britannia Secunda*, an area that stretched from the rivers Mersey to the Humber, and up to Hadrian's Wall. One of the off-shoots of this sub division was the fact that the gladiatorial games were split into four separate regional divisions, each with its own separate league. The winners of each league then played each other in a system of knock-out tournaments until a National Britannia League champion emerged. This Britannia champion was then automatically put forward to represent Britain in the larger European games. It is sad to reflect that Britain's teams never did very well in Europe. Sporting journalists of the time frequently remarked that British teams would insist on trying to run straight at their opponents with tridents, nets and javelins, whilst the Italians preferred the more effective approach of playing a long ball straight through the middle.

Britain, and *Eboracum*, were dragged into the dynastic turbulence of the Roman Empire some time around AD 306 when the Western Emperor named *Constantius* visited the town on his way north, to confiscate the Picts' ladders and make sure they kept to their side of the wall. Unfortunately when he arrived in *Eboracum* he promptly died, and hadn't even been feeling poorly. This was the second Roman Emperor to die in the city and, as a result no more Emperors ever risked visiting the city again, claiming that keeping hold of the job was difficult enough without paying a visit to "death wish city".

On the death of *Constantius* the Tetrarchy system declared that the ruling Emperor of the east, one *Flavius Valerius,* should be promoted to the vacant position. However the Legionnaires of York, being suspicious of someone whom they'd never worked with, and suspecting he was a foreigner, came up with a different idea. They went into a huddle and declared that the rightful Emperor of the West should be the son of *Constantius, Constantine,* who was already travelling to *Eboracum* after hearing that his fathers will was soon to be read. As soon as *Constantine* arrived in the city the Legionnaires made their declaration known and he accepted the job. Then, knowing what was good for him and only pausing to get hold of his inheritance, *Constantine* got out of the city as soon as possible.

However, the road to success is littered with stones, most of them with people's names and dates of birth carved on them. Over the next eighteen years all *Constantine's* rivals gradually disappeared, usually under large stones at the side of roads. Eventually, there being no other surviving rivals, *Constantine* was officially declared Emperor, and thus received the epithet "The Great".

Up to the reign of *Constantine,* Christianity had been just one of the many religious cults that was to be found in the eastern bit of the Empire, however after *Constantine* accepted the religion it went mega, spread throughout Europe, and ended up in *Eboracum.* The popularity of Christianity led to the building of many new temples, and the laying out of new cemeteries outside the town walls. Which in turn led to more streets being blocked and more traffic congestion, especially as the horse and carts taking the coffins to the new cemeteries went at such a slow pace.

By the large amount of Roman coffins and tombstones that have been found around the city it seems that death must have played a large part in the local economy. Undertakers and monumental masons must have been coining it in! When you come to think about it being a monumental mason in a society where most people couldn't read must have been a bit of a doddle. They could carve anything they wanted onto the tombs, and probably did.

The Romo-British society became even more refined and even gave birth to organisations into which people paid money. When they died, the organisation paid out, ensuring that the family of the dead person could afford to pay the funeral expenses. This system of life insurance is not unlike those wonderful companies of today that are advertised on afternoon television by those stalwarts of British broadcasting, Frank Windsor and Valerie Singleton. Although whether a Romo-Britain aged over 50 could get a policy without enduring a medical examination or even a salesman's visit is debatable.

The Romans also introduced into Britain a new concept in leisure pursuits - the wine bar. Up to this period of history the Britons only drank mead and a strong sort of black beer made from barley and herbs that tasted of old bushes. In fact in those days a public house was denoted by a bush hanging outside its doorway. Both these drinks were very potent and caused much drunkenness. It has to be remembered that as tea and coffee hadn't been discovered yet, the only thing to drink first thing in the morning was ale, the only thing to drink at lunch time was ale, the only thing to have with supper was ale, and the only place to go at night was the pub where they only sold ale. When you stop and think about it, it's no wonder that when the Romans were inventing civilization the Britons were painting themselves blue and charging around the country frightening each other. It's also worth noting that as soon as the Romans took over the country the first improvements they brought with them were wine, water conduits and sewers.

When the first wine bars opened they were treated with suspicion by the Britons and they avoided them like the plague, but slowly they became fashionable for the more trendy, upper class, "when in Rome do as the Romans do", sort of people. Eventually the place where you chose to drink became a cultural divide between the Romo-British and the True-Brits. Romo-Britons sat at little candlelit tables, nibbling roasted dormice and sipping wine whilst musicians played lutes in the background. True-Brits stood shoulder to shoulder in dark gloomy ale houses with sawdust on the table and not enough arm room to get your pint to your mouth, drinking warm beer all the while claiming that they would never be seen dead in a wine bar as they didn't serve a decent pint with a head on it, there was no dart board, and you couldn't get a decent pickled gherkin for love nor money.

As to be expected, after building a city and living there for around three hundred years, the Roman's left many remains behind. However, mainly due to the fact that stonemasons don't see much use in dragging large lumps of stone to a place where great piles of ready-cut stone are lying around already, combined with York's habit of continually re-building itself, much of the original Roman buildings were dismantled and recycled. However whilst the buildings might have been dismantled centuries ago, many Roman foundations are known to lie under the city, and many more may lie still undiscovered.

What with all the conservationists, archaeologists, preservationists, environmentalists, and recreationists all looking over their shoulder, it must be a very brave developer that suggests anything is ever built in the city again.

Over the years some remains and objects have been dug up and many bits and pieces have found their way into York's museums and gardens. In the late eighteenth century, a number of small Roman finds included a collection of bone and pottery counters, used by the Romans in a board game known as *ludus duodecium scriptorum,* a gambling game similar to a cross between ludo and snakes and ladders. As these finds were so near the fortress wall it is likely that they marked the site of an illegal gambling den, hidden out of sight of the authorities at the bottom of the ditch, where in the middle of the night the Roman soldiers and other citizens would huddle together in small groups to secretly play their games.

A number of small Dormouse bones were also found on the same site. This find indicates that the popular Roman snack of roasted dormouse, cooked in honey and coated with sunflower seeds, was readily available. Therefore it is possible to deduce that, as they played their illegal game, the gamblers were served by a food seller specialising in the fast food of the time. This food seller, one *Flavius Maximus,* noticed that the gamblers wouldn't go out if it rained at night, and so he built a small daub and wattle hut to protect the players from the inclement weather. Soon *Flavius Maximus* realised that he had a growing business on his hands. He did the hut up a bit, repainted it and hung a sign outside which read "Dunkin Dormice", thus founding the fast food industry.

Outside the fortress city the surrounding countryside was dotted with Roman estates and farms. The farms grew grain, and cattle, both dairy and beef herds. In the surrounding forests they farmed wild pigs, but some farms catered for the more discerning Roman palate. Latest research at an archeological site near Naburn shows that what once was thought to have been the remains of a Roman Villa have recently been revealed to be the remains of a Roman dormouse farm. The stone conduits originally thought to have been water and sewage ducts are in fact dormice runs. Fragments of small round cages have been revealed to be little wheels and balls similar to the ones we use today in hamster cages.

Throughout the latter half of the fourth century Rome suffered invasions, assassinations, new emperors, and a strange attack of enraged gibbons which seemed to have brought about the decline and fall of the Empire. Many of the troops that were stationed in Britain were needed back in Rome to defend the heart of the Empire in the mistaken belief that the lungs and stomach could look after themselves. Over the next few years more and more troops were taken from Britain.

As we all know from bitter personal experience, life is just like a game of snakes and ladders. When you think everything's going fine you step on a snake and before you know where you are, whoosh..... you're fifteen steps back from where you started. The frightening thing that is learnt by a study of history is that this snakes and ladders effect is not just confined to individuals. Sometimes it happens to groups of people, to villages, to towns, to cities, even to entire nations and empires and the Romo-British were just about to stand on the biggest snake of all.

As soon as the Roman hold on Britain was relaxed various waves of attackers sprung up and suddenly the country was under siege from all sides. In Scotland the Picts had been under attack from the Scotti who sailed from Ireland. As part of their defensive manoeuvres the Picts had learnt the art of wall climbing without ladders and, as soon as the Romans weren't looking, pushed south over Hadrian's Wall. Other tribes based in Southern Ireland began to attack Wales and the West Country. On the opposite side of England various waves of Jutes, Angles and Saxons sailed from Denmark and began attacking the east coast.

By AD 406, the native Romo-British, fed up of the comings and goings of a series of different Emperors, and equally fed up of the constant withdrawal of troops, and frequent attacks from all sides, eventually lost their rag, told Rome to stuff it and declared self rule.

In order to help defend themselves from the growing waves of attackers they had what they thought at the time, a very good idea. They employed foreign mercenaries to defend them. The only problem was that they employed mercenaries from the very same peoples that were attacking them, and what made matters even worse, once the mercenaries had done their job and seen everyone off, they decided to settle themselves. Thus Roman Britain came to an end and a new and bloody period of British history was about to begin.

CHAPTER TWO

EOFORWIC - ANGLO-SAXON YORK.

When the Roman Legionnaires finally departed from Britain the last one to leave turned the lights out after him. Hence the following period of British history is called The Dark Ages.

During this period the Romo-British citizens formed themselves into various independent British kingdoms, replacing the Roman administration, whilst the Saxons initially settled in the coastal areas. It was a period of turmoil, Celts fought Scotti, Scotti fought Picts, Picts fought Britons, Britons fought Saxons, and Saxons fought anyone left standing. Then, every so often, they would all gang up and fight each other. It was a period when life was cheap and rival factions competed against each other to come up with new and original ways to kill each other.

However, over the years without the Britons realising it, the Saxons spread inland. They did this in a very sneaky way, they would wait until no one was looking and then quietly in the middle of the night, move some miles inland, quickly knock up a daub and wattle hut, and then when daylight broke, swear blind that they had been there all the time. By means of these manoeuvres called "guerrilla settlement" the Saxons soon controlled large areas of land and established themselves into the Northumbrian kingdoms of Deira and Bernicia.

For almost a century the power struggle between the Saxons and Britons continued, but eventually the Saxons won by cheating even more. They deliberately gave themselves confusing names so that the Britons never knew who they were fighting. Saxon rulers sprang up with names like Aethelbald, Aethelbert, Aethelflaed, Athelfrith, Athelred, Aethelstan, and Athelwold. The Saxons also changed the names of many towns and villages, so that, as well as being confused about who they were meant to be fighting, the Britons were never quite sure where they should be fighting them. They never knew whether they were on their heads or their Athels. They lost many battles by default and eventually, becoming disheartened and totally fed up, they left the Saxons to get on with it and moved into Wales, thus becoming Welsh. Which probably explains a lot when you think about it.

It is claimed by some historians, and many writers of historical fiction, that the days of the legendary King Arthur, Camelot and the Knights of the Round Table were supposed to be early medieval. Modern research tells us a different story. It now shows that Arthur was a war leader of the Britons, fighting a rear guard action against the Saxon newcomers around the dates AD 490 -520.

Today, despite there being a virtual publishing industry based upon Arthurian novels, archaeological claims and counter claims, and other assorted writings, computer games, T-shirts and musical pageants, any definite traces of this elusive King are few and far between. This was probably due to the fact that he was not successful. He lost the battle for England. It is a sad fact of life that societies tend to build statues and monuments to their successful people. They very rarely commemorate failure. For instance, scattered throughout Britain are many monuments and memorials to the manager and team of the England World Cup winning squad of 1966. History will forever remember the names of Sir Alf Ramsey, Nobby Stiles, Bobby and Jackie Charlton, Geoff Hurst and Bobby Moore. By comparison the English supporters of more recent times are still trying to forget the name of Graham Taylor. Will his name be remembered a thousand years from now? I very much doubt it.

It is believed that *Eboracum* fell to the Saxons around AD 593. The Saxons had been watching the city for some time and noticed that once a year most of the inhabitants left the city for a works outing to the coast. One year the Saxons waited until everyone had gone out and then snuck into the deserted town. As soon as the Saxons got inside the city they promptly added it to their kingdom of Deira and renamed it Eoforwic, a Saxon word meaning "How's your fathers goat?"

They very quickly changed all sign posts and when the native Britons returned from their trip to the coast, they couldn't find *Eboracum* any more. It had simply ceased to exist. Finally, after wandering around for a while with puzzled looks on their faces, they travelled south and took refuge in the British Kingdom of Elmete.

By AD 600 the spread of the Saxons across Northern England was just about complete, and everyone began to settle down and get on with the job of building up society once again. However, due to the culture clash between the native Romo-British and the Saxons, everyone worshipped different deities. Some native people were Christian, some still hung onto the Roman gods, half the troops worshipped Mithras, whilst the Saxon newcomers worshipped such gods as Woden, Tiw the god of war, and Frig the Goddess of love and mother of men. Indeed some of our names for days of the week are still named after those Saxon gods. Tuesday is named after Tiw, Wednesday after Woden, Thursday after Thor and Friday after Frig (as in "Frig it, it's the weekend, I'm off home!").

It is interesting to note that no days of the weekend or Mondays were named after Saxon gods. Two lines of thought have developed about this. The first theory is that the Saxons didn't believe in weekends either long or short and just worked through from Tuesday to Tuesday. The second theory is that they always took the weekend off, got drunk, woke up Monday morning feeling lousy and went back to bed until Tiwsday.

There were lots of other Dark Age gods, and there are still traces of them around. Easter is named after the Saxon god Eostre, the god of chocolate eggs. The once Christian feast day of Lammastide, celebrated on 1st August was derived from the Saxon hlafmasse, meaning loaf time, a time when bread was made from the first corn. Obviously this celebration has died out in modern times with the development of winter wheat and round the year crop growth.

This multi-god situation eventually got so out of hand that just about every day of the week was a celebration of some sort, dedicated to many lesser gods of both the Saxons and the Romo-British. Soon the local population twigged onto the fact that if they followed all religions it was possible to enjoy a bank holiday three hundred and sixty five days of the year.

The rest of Europe saw what was happening in Britain and decided that it did not comply to the dictates of the Social Charter, an EC law that decreed that someone, somewhere must work some of the time. They complained to the Pope and in consequence he dispatched a Bishop Augustine to England to sort things out.

Augustine arrived in Canterbury, and pronounced himself Archbishop, then he recruited some helpers and set about teaching the English to follow Christianity - the one true religion. One of Augustine's helpers was a Bishop called Paulinus who came up with the good idea that instead of converting the population one at a time, it would be a better idea to convert their kings and then every one else under the King would have to follow. It worked - many English Kings were converted, and their followers and subjects converted accordingly.

However not all the peasantry were happy about this change, mainly because with only "one true religion", they got a lot fewer bank holidays. As they quite rightly pointed out, as far as the King was concerned every day was a holiday. But there was no arguing the point. In the Dark Ages there was one Golden Rule that simply stated, "Them what has the gold gets to rule!" and there was no appeal. Hence the spread of Christianity increased and the worship of any other Gods was frowned upon.

In AD 617 a bloke called Edwin took control of the Anglian Kingdom of Deira and, for the next eight years, set about strengthening and expanding his kingdom until he controlled all of Northumbria. Once he had established his power base it was deemed that it was time for him to take a wife. This was despite him having a wife and two children already for, some years before whilst he was in Mercia, he married Cwenburh, the daughter of King Cearl. In these days of rival kingdoms, and rulers with a thirst for conquest, it was the norm for kings to enter into political marriages which would help to strengthen their position. Some kings would cast aside their previous relationship, some would continue it. Some even married and never saw their new wives, preferring things to stay as they were. It seems that the Roman

Church must have had a more sympathetic policy when it came to dealing with divorced kings in those days.

History is a bit vague about what happened to Cwenburh after Edwin decided that he could do a lot worse than arrange a marriage link to the strong Anglian Kingdom of Kent. King Ethelbert of Kent had an eligible daughter, Ethelburga, sister to Hamburga, Sesameseedburga, and Chiliburga, and so the appropriate arrangements were made. However there was one draw back. Ethelburga was a Christian, and Edwin was still unconverted, but true love and politics have a habit of negotiating most obstacles and Edwin agreed to allow his new wife to follow her Christian practices.

The power of love and politics sometimes creates strange bedfellows (for more information on this subject read any of today's tabloid newspapers), and two years later Edwin agreed to be baptized in a small wooden church that had been especially built for the occasion next to his own palace in Eoforwic. Obviously once their king had been baptized the rest of the kingdom had to follow and for a number of months Christian converts, led by Paulinus walked around Deira dragging the local population out of their hovels and throwing them into the nearest river, stream or duck pond. When they re-surfaced, coughing and spluttering, they were pronounced Christians. This process was called baptism. Soon, as well as suffering from colds and rheumatism, the entire kingdom was Christian, a situation that led to important ramifications for Eoforwic. Edwin made the city the capital of his Kingdom and Paulinus made the town a centre of his ecclesiastical endeavours in the North of England.

In AD 633 Edwin managed to get himself killed in the battle of Hatfield, and throughout the following year, the Northumbrian Kingdom was fought over and pulled apart by rival factions. Edwin's wife saw the writing on the wall. It read "Take steps!" and so she, her kids and Paulinus, took steps - bloody long steps right out of Northumbria - and fled back to Kent.

With all of Edwin's immediate family back down south the kingdom was divided into two once again. The only family member who had stayed behind, one Osric, son of Edwin's Uncle, ruled over Deira, and Eanfrith, son of Athelfrith, took control of Bernicia. As soon as they came to power they both renounced the Christian faith and Cadwallon, taking revenge for Edwin throwing him out of Gwynedd, promptly invaded Northumbria and killed them.

However a second son of Athelfrith, one Oswald, who was next in line for Bernicia, fought Cadwallon at Hexham. Having the home advantage proved decisive and he gave Cadwallon a jolly good stuffing. This home victory elevated Oswald to the top job in both kingdoms and so Northumbria was united once again.

It has to be said that, in a period of very silly names such as Athlefrith, Athelfruth, and Athlefroth, the name Oswald was a truly silly name for a powerful ruler. It is noted with interest that it has never been seriously considered as a suitable name for a King again, the English monarchy preferring to stick with the more traditional names such as Henry, James, George, and Edward.

Being of "Geordie" heritage Oswald preferred to rule his kingdom from further north and the royal court left Eoforwic to establish their headquarters at Bamburgh. In AD 634 he invited Bishop Aidan from the Christian monastery on the Scottish island of Iona to Northumbria for a long weekend. Being an "island" sort of person Aidan took one look at the island of Lindisfarne and fell in love with the place. As soon as the tide went out he took his packed lunch, walked across the sandy causeway and established a monastery on the island. Lindisfarne Monastery would soon play a large role in the Christian world, with its influence being felt throughout Europe.

For the next hundred or so years the Kingdom of Northumbria saw a series of kings come and go. Some died in suspicious circumstances, some died with a variety of enemy weapons stuck in them, very few died in their beds.

Oswald was killed at the battle of Maserfeld in AD 642 by Penda, King of Mercia. It is said that his death gave a name to the nearby town of Oswestry. It seems that it was named after something called Oswald's

Tree, a reference to the way the king met his bloody end. It is said that after the battle his body was hacked to pieces and the various dismembered bits were stuck on the end of spears that were stuck into the ground. From a distance this gruesome sight resembled a tree, hence the name. Remember what we said about new and original ways to kill each other? Oswald's was by far the most inventive.

In later years it was claimed that this bit of land became a holy site due to the fact that a horse suffering from colic was cured by eating some blood soaked soil and then went on to win the Cheltenham Gold Cup at very long odds.

This hacking about of Oswald's body, plus a 14/1 winner, brought about a great boost in the trade of religious relics. It is recorded that Oswald's right arm ended up in Peterborough, his left arm in Gloucester, and a third one in Durham! His head was claimed to have been at Durham, and somewhere in Luxemburgh. Winchester claimed his two left feet, Canterbury claimed one right foot and a left hand, whilst his entire body was meant to have been at St. Winnoc's in Flanders. If one goes through the historic claims of various European churches and abbeys that claimed to have a bit of Oswald one can only come to the conclusion that the man must have either have had more limbs than a centipede or that someone, somewhere was making a very good living telling porkies and selling forgeries.

York has one monument to this multi-limbed King. St. Oswald's Hall on Fulford Road was originally a Norman chapel, and contains some fine medieval woodcarvings. However the site is much older as excavations revealed both Roman and Saxon remains. However there is no record of the building ever claiming to have any bit of Oswald's body.

After Oswald's death, Osric's son Oswin returned to Deira as ruler whilst Bernicia passed onto Oswy, son of Athelfrith. As Oswy's power grew he attempted to unite the two kingdoms. He challenged Oswin to battle but Oswin, being a sensible sort of bloke, refused. It was to no avail as in AD 651 Oswy, miffed at Oswin's refusal to face him in battle, arranged to have him successfully assassinated. In his place he put his own nephew and Oswald's son, Athelwold, onto the Bernician throne.

Oswy was then attacked by Penda, who seemed to have a thing about Northumbria, but this final attack proved his last as he was defeated by Oswy and his son Athelfrith at the battle of Winwaed, during which Athelfrith was killed. For services rendered Oswy promoted his son as ruler of Bernicia, but for reasons best known to himself Athelfrith rebelled against his father and was never heard of again.

All this coming and going caused the inhabitants of Northumbria a great deal of confusion due to the fact that they were never too sure who was ruling them and from where. One week it was a large, axe waving bloke with a forked beard and a war band based in Bamburgh. The next week it was by some distant relative of his with a sharper axe, a longer forked beard and bigger war band, who was based down somewhere down south near Doncaster.

At first a local trade in the making and selling of commemorative mugs and sundry tableware sprang up, but the rulers came and went so quickly that, by the time the potter had the things made and distributed, there was a new king on the throne and his stock was out of date. They decided to concentrate on the more usual "Present from Eoforwic" pottery thimbles instead.

As the local population never really knew what was going on they lost all track of time and, when Oswy quietened things down a bit, it was discovered that they were celebrating their Easter bank holiday at a different time from the rest of the world. Remembering the Northumbrian talent for celebrations the Roman Church quickly stepped in once again and decided that there should be a meeting to sort it all out before it got out of hand.

This meeting, known as the Synod of Whitby, was held, surprisingly enough, at Whitby under Oswy's chairmanship. The date of Easter was decided and Northumbria was brought into line with the rest of Europe. This action annoyed the Northumbrian people who could now only have the one bank holiday so to placate them the European Community arranged for them to be given a selection of gaily wrapped chocolate eggs. A tradition still carried out by chocolate manufacturers today.

In AD 670 Oswy became unique in the annals of the Kings of Northumbria when he fell ill and promptly died in his bed. There followed a series of kings who came and went in quick succession. Kings such as Eadwulf, Osred, Coenred, Osric, Ceolwulf, Eadberht, Oswulf, Athelwold Moll, Alhred, Athelred, Alfwald, Osred, Osbald & Eardwulf. All that lot ruled Northumbria between 705 and 810, more than fourteen rulers in a hundred years. With an average reign of seven years each, being King was certainly not the long term career prospect it seems today, and the life insurance premiums must have been enormous.

Whilst this game of musical thrones was being played, Northumbria itself was undergoing a renaissance of learning, led by the church. This was due to two factors. Firstly the various kings and their war bands were always declaring war on each other and fighting dreadful battles, and secondly there were very few job options open to young people. If you didn't have a trade, it was either the army or the monastery and a lot of the brighter kids noticed that many of the people who joined the army didn't come back, so, not liking the idea of their bodily extremities being cut off and stuck on bits of trees, they went for the longer term career option and entered into the monasteries.

This was a fortunate thing for the church, who suddenly finding themselves inundated by bright intelligent young men, got them on reading, writing, and painting as soon as they walked through the doors. This was the foundation course from where career minded young monks progressed to learn the businesses of advanced painting, manuscript illumination, brewing, gardening, bee keeping and sheep farming. The more intellectually gifted amongst them studied medicine and the growing of herbs, and went around the countryside solving crimes and eventually had crime novels and television programmes written about them.

Some monks even progressed onto the really advanced subjects of comparative religion and politics, qualifications that allowed them to dabble in the affairs of statecraft. Indeed some of them became so proficient that they found themselves advisers to kings and their courts throughout Europe. Some proved good at the job whilst others succumbed to the temptations of the flesh, and became rich and powerful. The antithesis of what they were trained to do, but that's what education can do for you!

Whilst warfare raged up and down the country, and sometimes from side to side, the monks got on with things and by the time everyone came to realise it, the monasteries controlled many flourishing businesses and grew, owned, traded or sold nearly everything there was to grow, own, trade or sell.

The more sensitive and creative monks specialised in art and great strides forward were made in the study and practice of the creative arts, including rafia work. The Northumbrian monasteries also specialised in the design and production of things called Illuminated Manuscripts. These were books that were very similar in concept to today's "graphic novels", an intellectual name for comic books that makes them more acceptable for booksellers to stock. Monks would spend hours of labour tracing, drawing out and colouring in these manuscripts, which were mainly biblical works, religious tracts and lives of saints.

As the general populace was illiterate, once they were written, these manuscripts were given to kings as important gifts which they highly valued. The kings would leave them lying around just to impress people and to give the impression that they could read. In consequence these manuscripts became the first "coffee table books", books that are doomed to lie around unread but looking good and saying that their owners are not only intellectuals but also people of impeccable taste.

Many of these illuminated manuscripts eventually ended up in the Minster Library at Eoforwic which, as the general population couldn't read, had very few visitors and in consequence was a very quiet place. This quiet atmosphere became the norm for all libraries of the time and thus became the origin of the tradition that all libraries should be quiet places.

But what about Eoforwic itself? With all the military coming and going the church had kept its head down and, without anyone really noticing, established the City as an ecclesiastical centre. St. Wilfrid, a pupil of Aidan's at Lindisfarne, came to Eoforwic and was made bishop in AD 669. It is recorded that he was bad tempered and rarely got on with anyone, which, when you think about it, made him just the person for such a job!

His CV is a careers officer's nightmare and tells a sorry tale. Employed in AD 669, he was sacked in AD 677, reinstated in AD 686 and sacked again in AD 691. However, whilst he held the job down, he did manage to arrange the repair of Edwin's small church and laid the foundations for today's more grand Minster.

Another religious leader was the famous vegetarian monk, Egbutnobacon. He was established as Archbishop of York in AD 735 and soon made the city the intellectual centre of Northumbria. He rebuilt Wilfrid's minster, facing his new building east to west, and established the world famous minster school and library. More importantly he introduced the concept of vegetarianism to a population more used to chewing on great hunks of spit roasted meat.

To persuade the population to take him seriously Egbutnobacon came up with the great idea of spreading a rumour around the north of England that all the cows had gone mad, and if the people ate enough of them they would go mad as well. As the rumour spread and people began to look for something else to chew on he experimented in making special types of vegetarian food in the kitchens of the Minster Library.

He developed a vegeburger, a vegetarian cottage pie made with real cottages, vegetarian carrot sausages, and a number of other prepacked vegetarian items. However, in a meat eating society where all restaurants were strictly carvery only with no salad bar, they never really caught on. Eventually his secret recipes were sent back to

Scotland, to the monastery of Iona, where they remained hidden for some centuries until they were discovered by the photographer, keyboard player and vegetarian gourmet, (the sadly late), Linda McCartney.

York has very few remains from this period of its history. One is the church of St. Mary's Bishophill where the distinctive Saxon herring bone style of brick laying can clearly be seen. Why the Saxons chose to lay their bricks in this style is unknown, after all, anyone can tell you that it's far easier to lay bricks one top of each other. As with most historic enigmas, a number of wild and diverse theories have been put forward as an explanation. One, put forward by the famous 19th century cleric, hand knitter and rug maker, the Rev Readicut, claimed that the patterns of the bricks were based on the famous Saxon hand knitted pullovers that originated on the North East Coast.

Another theory claimed that the Saxons could never put their scaffolding up straight and so their brickwork was doomed from the start. Yet another theory claims that the original brickwork was actually normal, but sometime during the latter half of the 14th century York experienced a slight earth tremor which dislodged the bricks, making them fall into the positions they are in today.

Without doubt the most important archeological find from this period is the famous Jorvik Pudding Basin, now to be seen in the Castle Museum, and which some historians claim is a warrior's helmet. However they are sadly mistaken. If this so called helmet is turned upside down its true purpose can clearly be seen. The helmet is shaped so that it fits happily on a stove or over a fire. What is claimed to be the nose piece is actually the pudding basin handle. The cheek plates form a sort of folded lid, whilst the chain mail is obviously a perfect example of an early anti-splash guard.

This theory backs up a little known fact about the Anglo Saxons, that they were famous for their puddings. Indeed it is claimed that they invented many of today's famous British puddings. Their major culinary achievement occurred around AD 580 when Aethelstrudelsson, the nine year old son of Aethelstrudel, refused to eat his bread. "If you don't eat it up you'll get it for your pudding young man!" his mother said. And sure enough he did, an event that gave birth to the famous bread and butter pudding.

The infamous "spotted dick" also originates from this period, however it seems that this was more likely the name of a strange disease that was cured by pouring hot custard over the persons infected parts. After this disease was successfully wiped out it was commemorated by the invention of a pudding, still traditionally served with hot custard.

One of the reasons that not many remains from the Saxon period still survive is that Saxons were not very good builders. Despite Eoforwic being a capital city most of the population lived in small villages and hamlets in the surrounding area. In the town itself daub and wattle huts and wooden halls were built over the Roman remains and a number of small timber churches constructed. Little stone was used with the exception of the Minister. The Roman barracks were used, mainly to house troops and war bands, as were many of the existing paved Roman streets but, during this period, the centre of the city shifted towards the space between the Ouse and the Foss. This shift of emphasis was due to the establishment of a market nearer to the landing stages on the river. All the building and rebuilding caused a great deal of upset, and as usual, all the roads and streets were blocked again. This upset all the market traders so much that they got together and opened up further down the road.

Eoforwic was an important port, with an important market place. Many goods were imported and exported. Trade developed and the market place grew. Many stalls did brisk business, others tried to sell Egbutnobacon's vegetarian pies and pasties. The successful traders soon grew rich and moved into the larger Roman houses and villas which was a practical solution to any housing shortage. Let's face it you wouldn't spend time and money building a place of your own if there was a ready supply of superior built dwellings that just needing a bit of doing up waiting empty for you. You wouldn't go to the time and trouble of building your own hut if there was a second hand Barratt house standing empty next door, or would you? This system of rehabitation has since been echoed in pre-war years by many inner city rejuvenation projects.

CHAPTER THREE

JORVIK - VIKING YORK.

It is a well known fact of life that just when you've got something the way you want it, just when you feel it's safe to sit back and put your feet up, that's the moment when the shit chooses to hit the fan and, in AD 867, a very big lump hit a very big fan in a very big way.

Whilst the Saxons were getting on with important things like farming and inventing new puddings, a Viking leader named Ivar the Boneless sailed a Viking army of 350 ships from East Anglia, up the North Sea, along the Humber and up the Ouse till he reached Eoforwic. On his way he dropped off a land army at Barton-on-Humber who marched overland and approached the town from the opposite side of the river.

The following morning when the occupants of Eoforwic woke up there was a line of Viking warships that stretched for four miles down the river, all bristling with large hairy warriors. When they looked out of their back windows they saw a second army, of even larger hairy warriors standing outside the walls leaning on their war shields and picking their teeth with large axes. Sneakily, before the occupants of the town even had the chance to make a cup of tea, the Vikings rushed into the city and there was a ferocious battle. As the Vikings well knew the inhabitants were useless without their morning cuppa and very soon threw their weapons down and handed the keys of the city to Ivar, not caring whether he was boneless or not.

As soon as they held the city the Vikings, in a move designed to confuse any Saxons foolish enough to come back, changed the town's name to Jorvik. Despite having a reputation for murder, mayhem, rape and pillage many Vikings were settlers and the more sedate members of the army settled down, rebuilt and expanded the city, whilst the more hairy arsed and berserk of the warriors marched off down south looking for murder, mayhem, rape and pillage. Which they found in large quantities.

Nothing really changed much in Jorvik during the Viking occupation. Despite having a new name the same things were done by the same people. The place might be ruled by Vikings now, but it was still the same poor bloke that shovelled the same shit, and it was still the same towns folk that ran the all day breakfast cafe bars, albeit they now served pickled herring at breakfast, lunch and tea. The city was constantly re-built with old buildings being condemned and re-juvenated, new huts erected and, as usual, the roads and pavements were blocked up everywhere.

The market was moved back into the centre of the city and the main docks were re-positioned on the Ouse where the present day Kings Staith stands. This move created the need for the building and naming of many new streets and the present day streets of York still bear the names given to them by the Vikings. Goodramgate, the street where Good's ram was penned behind a stout gate. Micklegate, the main road leading in and out of the city, named because it was always being rebuilt and in a constant state of confusion or "Mickle", as in the old saying of "many a mickle makes a muckle". What sort of thing a muckle actually was, or precisely how many mickles went into it has been lost to time, which is, perhaps, a good thing.

It was once estimated by someone who had more time on their hands than they knew what to do with, that over forty York street names ended in the word "gate", a Viking word meaning street, which only goes to show what an unimaginative lot the Vikings were. However, despite the quaint daub and wattle huts set amongst the picturesque Roman ruins the town was anything but attractive. No one had thought to plant the walls with daffodils back then. It was cold, damp and muddy in winter, and warm, damp and muddy in summer. The houses all had a crude form of central heating, a fire in the middle of the living area. However as the Vikings hadn't figured out how to build chimneys, there was no pushing the damper in and pulling the damper out cos the smoke just went all over the house just the same. It drifted up to the ceilings and hung around in great grey clouds until someone opened a door. Indeed when the fire was going in those days it was quite possible to sit all alone inside your house and, when someone opened the door and the smoke drifted out, discover that half the street had come in and were warming themselves at the other side of the room.

Next door to each house was a space just big enough to keep a few pigs, which must have helped the sanitation problem no end. However as dustbins and dustbin men hadn't been invented yet it was a good way to get rid of the household waste, and the resulting manure ensured that at least the inhabitants had a good crop of rhubarb every year.

Despite the Romans leaving behind their drains and sewers the Vikings preferred a more crude sort of ablution. Many of them preferred to simply crap in holes that they dug in the ground, some never even bothered to dig the hole. Their idea of an air freshener was a pig on a string. As a result the city stank to high heaven. After his visit Egil, a visitor from Iceland wrote "Jorvik -the danke demesne". If he thought that and he came from Iceland we can only assume that the demesne must have been very danke indeed!

The remains of this Viking city were revealed during the world famous Coppergate excavations. This archaeological dig, which lasted for over five years, produced Britain's richest source of remains from this period. The wooden timber foundations of many houses and workshops were uncovered which in turn yielded up items of jewellery, bonework, shoes, tools, and cooking utensils. But out of all the 15,000 small remains the most famous and most popular with York visitors is the legendary Jorvik Turd.

Today this strange little item can be seen, encased in plastic, inside the Jorvik Viking Centre, at Coppergate, probably less than a hundred yards from where it first squeezed its way out of a Viking bottom. It is one of the finest examples of historic human excrement ever found, rivalling even the famous Golden Turd of Sutton Hoo that can be seen in the British Museum.

When this artefact was first found a great debate raged as to who it once belonged to. Some archaeologists claimed that it actually belonged to Eric Bloodaxe, some claimed that it was owned by a later king Olav Gothfrithson, whilst others claimed it was not a male turd at all but was dropped by a female bottom.

Eventually, after a long period of examination by a team of governmental crap experts employed by the Ministry of Agriculture Food and Fisheries, (M.A.F.F.), the argument was finally settled. Having studied nothing but crap for many years their expertise was finally able to determine that the turd had no royal connections at all but once belonged to Eric Leanshanksforkibeard the owner of the Olde Jorvik Kebab Shoppe, who dropped it behind a hedge one Friday night on his way back home from the pub.

One of the small business establishments uncovered during the Coppergate dig was a shop owned by a Viking named Eric the Slightly Blue. He was a warrior merchant, given his name because he was very susceptible to the cold, and because he was a supporter of free enterprise. We can find a trace of him in the Icelandic sagas written in the 12th century by the Icelandic historian Snorri Snorrisson, ancestor of Magnus Magnusson.

> *"And thus Eric the Slightly Blue sailed from his Norse homelands, eventually to settle at Jorvik, where he began to ply a strange trade of selling small olde worlde crafties and gifties."*

It was said of Eric the Slightly Blue that he was so mean he would sell a blind man a rat's arse as a wedding ring, but second hand jewellery was only one of his ventures. He also made a grizzly living selling Saint's relics, and had the most original "second hand" shop in York. As well as second hands it also sold second legs and other sundry, saintly bits and pieces. It was Eric who sold the arm of St. Giles of the Golden Frog to Winchester Cathedral and who sold the leg of St. Ledger of the Steeplechase to Canterbury Cathedral. He was inspired by the story of St. Oswald and once, at the height of his career, stocked no fewer than four St. Oswald legs, two St. Oswald hands, both left ones, and a piece of left buttock .

One day whilst he was trying to fulfil a special commission to find the Magical Bum of St. Barnabus the Flatulent, his business partner, an unfortunate man called Tommy, who had only one leg and one arm and who was also deaf, dumb and blind, decided to get out of the business whilst he still could, and fled the city. Consequently Eric was forced into bankruptcy claiming that the bottom had fallen out of his business.

Another occupant of the city was a Viking named Lethal Ferkinburgerbender, the son of Ethel Burgerbender. Records of this Viking can also be found in the sagas written by Snorri Snorrisson. It is believed that, shortly after seeing an unfortunate accident between a village dog and a passing ox wagon, he was the first butcher who discovered how to produce a strange round, flattened sausage that would fit easier in the strange round flattened bread buns that the Viking bakers produced.

This new quick snack soon caught on with the Viking warriors who, what with all the murder, mayhem, rape and pillage, rarely got around to cooking for themselves and instantly took to the concept of fast food. Soon Lethal had a chain of fast food wagons travelling to all the major battles and which became known as "Ferkinburgerbenderbars". Viking warriors, as they camped around the glowing fires of yet another burning Saxon village were often heard to mutter the immortal words "Just what the hell is in these Ferkinburgers!"

The Vikings also introduced a number of different sports and past times into England, one of which was ice skating. Archaeological evidence shows that the Vikings made their ice skates from animal bones that were strapped to the bottom of their leather boots. When the river froze they would strap on their skates and whiz up and down the frozen ice, thus giving birth to the great tradition of English ice skaters such as John Curry and Torvill'n Dean.

After the Coppergate site was excavated the large hole left in the ground was converted into "The Jorvik Viking Centre" a museum dedicated to the Viking city. It incorporates actual Viking remains within the reconstruction of a Viking street that can be seen by the paying public via a seated ride in a golf cart with the voice of Magnus Magnusson speaking in your ear.

Under Viking rule, life carried on regardless in Jorvik and the city expanded. By the 880's the city was a major trading centre with direct trade routes to the Viking Kingdoms of Norway, Dublin, Denmark and the Low Countries. The occupants of the city returned to Christianity and things settled down for a few years.

However, in AD 927 confusion once more gained the upper hand. The English King Athelstan annexed York and there followed twenty eight years of battle, mayhem and turmoil. Out of this confusion steps the figure of Eric Bloodaxe whom history refers to as "a colourful character". A statement that usually disguises the fact that the person was a right bastard! And so he was: even the Vikings own records describe him as being "a bad-minded, gruff, unfriendly, and silent man". It is believed that he eventually became the patron saint of nightclub bouncers.

He took over the city of Jorvik in AD 947 and managed to upset so many people that he got himself expelled the following year. He spent a lot of time raping, pillaging and getting drunk and then came back again in AD 952, and did it all over again with the result that he got expelled once again, this time in AD 954. Someone told him the saying "third time lucky" so he gathered an army together and was just about to try again when someone decided enough was enough and murdered him. That put an end to any Viking attempt to recapture the city and the Viking Kingdom of Jorvik finally became part of England.

Once it was part of England, as usual, the name of the city changed again, and Jorvik became York, the name it has enjoyed for the last thousand years. The city, instead of being a capital of a northern kingdom, became the capital of a northern earldom. This fact meant very little to the inhabitants who still had to pay their taxes and their tithes to some bloke that lived in the big house on top of the hill. In fact when you think about it the lot of the common man didn't change much for hundreds of years, and still hasn't! Another fine example of the previously mentioned "Golden Rule" carrying on through the ages.

CHAPTER FOUR

1066 And All That.

The Vikings, and to some extent the Saxons, viewed the succession of kingdoms and thrones with a certain amount of flexibility. As we have already noted usually, on the death of the incumbent, the throne was taken over by the bloke who had the sharpest axe and the biggest army. The English rulers had a different system, one of hereditary succession. The question of which is the correct way to choose someone to rule over a country is not a subject that this author wishes to pursue in this book. However when you look at some of the hereditary peers that sit in the present day House Of Lords, there is something to be said for the system with the big bloke with the sharpest axe. Which ever system was chosen it was bound to upset someone, and in the year 1066 the system of succession managed to upset just about everyone there was to upset.

Throughout the reign of Ethelred II, England was continuously attacked by Viking armies. They would wait until the King was looking in the opposite direction and then sneak ashore from their great long boats, beat the hell out of anyone they came across, and grab as much land and plunder as they could. These frequent events led to Ethelred being given the name of "The Unready". When one of the king's own sons, Edmund Ironsides named after his monumentally large thighs, was killed in battle in 1016 Ethelred, believing that discretion was the better part of valour, fled the country and took exile in Normandy among his wife's family.

For a brief period England was ruled by a Danish King Canute, who, when he died, passed the kingdom onto his son Harthacnut. However the family line ended there. There were no Quartercnuts nor even any Hardliacnuts, so Harthacnut made Edward, a surviving son of exiled King Ethelred, the heir.

The following summer Harthacnut went to the wedding of his personal standard bearer, a bloke called Tofig the Proud, however the wedding reception was ruined when Harthacnut choked on a bit of wedding cake and promptly died, a fact that might seem, under the circumstances, just a bit fishy to some suspicious minded people.

Hence in 1042 , Edward, son of Ethelred II, ascended to the throne of England. Due to his curious, self effacing habit of taking the blame when anything went wrong he became known as Edward the Confessor. If the annual harvest failed Edward would tell everyone it was his fault. If plague broke out he took the responsibility. He blamed himself for the weather, diseases, bad economy, outbreaks of warts, infestations of newts and for all the other little everyday disasters that happened to anyone under his reign. Which was fine by the other English lords, barons and anyone else who held the remotest bit of responsibility. If they screwed up they just blamed Edward, and Edward being Edward, happily took the blame. Americans have a great name for people like this - they call them shmucks!

Due to his virtually constant state of undergoing confession, Edward's knees became fixed into a kneeling position, which made sitting on a throne difficult to say the least. Finally, in order to atone for everything being his fault, he devoted all his energies to building a great church at Westminster. It was consecrated in the December of 1065 but unfortunately the King was too ill to attend. His illness got worse and he spent a rotten Christmas. He had an even worse New Year as, on January 5th 1066, he died. He did however have the very great honour of being the first person to be interred in his new Westminster Abbey.

Despite it being expected, Edward's death left the country in some confusion. During his stay in Normandy some years earlier he had proclaimed Duke William of Normandy as his successor. After he returned to England he controlled the country through a system of barons, lords, and earls. One of these Earls came from the family of Godwinson, the Earls of Wessex, a family linked to the Danish Kings of England. Whilst Edwin concentrated on his confessions and religious works this family looked after the day to day running of the country. Eventually they found themselves more or less running the place. As

Edward fell ill it was more or less assumed that the sons of Godwinson, the Earls Harold and Tostig would be the natural successors to the English throne. Indeed with the exception of the fact that no one would take the blame anymore, no one would really notice any difference.

During Edward's reign Tostig had become the Earl of Northumbria and had established his headquarters in York. However he turned out to be a right old bugger. He was an Earl of the old school and firmly believed in giving his peasants as hard a time as possible. After suffering from his maltreatment for a number of years the peasants got fed up, organised themselves, ganged up, and chucked him out of York. Tostig immediately went to his elder brother and asked him to persuade the King reinstate his earldom, but Harold, being a stickler for proper behaviour, backed the King. Tostig kicked up such a fuss about this that eventually he got himself banished and immediately sailed off to Normandy to see Duke William who was unimpressed by his story and sent him back off again. Now in a right sulk Tostig sailed around the English coast for a while before ending up in Norway at the court of King Harald Hardrada. Meanwhile Northumbria was put in the hands of the brothers of Harold's wife, the Earls Edwin and Morcar.

As we have already said, on the death of Edward it was generally assumed that Harold would ascend to the English thorn. However the people in the know had their money on a horse of a much different colour. They knew that Edward the Confessor had actually promised the Kingdom to William Duke of Normandy, and they watched Harold's rise to power with more than a deal of interest. They supported his cause, not through any great love of Danish Kings and their families, but mainly because, like most English people, they had an intense dislike of the French. As the body of Edwin the Confessor was lowered into its tomb in his own Abbey, at one end of the building, Harold was busy having himself crowned King at the other. The entire country held its breath and, keeping an eye on the south coast, quickly buried everything they had of value and began sharpening their swords, spears and axes.

Harold gathered his forces in the south and waited all through the summer of 1066, but when the first attack came on English shores, true to the family tradition set by Ethelred the Unready, it turned out he was looking the wrong way and was about three hundred miles too far south.

Tostig, ever eager to ingratiate himself with someone who would listen to him, had finally managed to persuade the Norwegian king that England, especially York, was a ripe fruit just ready for picking! Actually he didn't. That was just a bit of prose that real history books seem to rely on. Tostig and Hardrada never spoke in metaphors. They spoke more directly. Tostig turned up at the Norwegian court knowing full well that two years previously Hardrada had declared peace with their Swedish neighbours and ever since the Viking army had sat on their behinds, sharpening their axes and waiting for someone to fight. By the time he turned up the axes were so sharp and the Vikings so wound up that they were about to fight amongst themselves.

He had a chat with Harald Hardrada and before much longer the Vikings were packing up their travel gear, kissing their wives and kids good-bye and singing to themselves the well known marching chant of "Here we go, here we go, here we go!"

This huge Viking army sailed from Norway, picked up more forces in the Orkneys and sailed down the East Coast of England. After attacking Scarborough for no other reason than it was there they took the familiar route up the Humber and along the Ouse until they saw the walls of York. They disembarked at Riccall, just down river, and marched towards the city. The Northumbrians quickly gathered their forces and, led by Earls Edwin and Morcar, met the invaders at Fulford.

By the time they reached England this Viking army was the largest ever assembled. It comprised over three hundred ships, each holding around eighty to one hundred warriors. Not only did it contain the army of the King of Norway, it also contained the Kings of the Orkneys, Iceland and Dublin, and their armies. It was no great surprise that the Northumbrian Lords Edwin and Morcar were utterly defeated. What is amazing is the fact that they considered marching out to meet it at all.

The Vikings easily captured the city but for reasons best known to themselves, they didn't take immediate occupation. Instead the victorious army demanded hostages and allowed the city four days to yield up five hundred of its men at a place called Stamford Bridge, just outside York. Then they marched off back to their boats for a bit of rest and recreation, with, no doubt, some rape and pillage on the side.

News that York had fallen soon reached Harold and in a march that equals any great march in history, he travelled up the A1 and along the A64. Without even bothering to stop at a Little Chef, he reached the outskirts of York the evening of the fourth day, the night before the hostages were due to be handed over at Stamford Bridge. That night, under cover of darkness, his army crept into the city. The following morning they marched out again.

The Vikings, who were enjoying a bit of quality leisure time by swimming in the river, playing football, and having a picnic (relaxations still enjoyed by Norwegians today), were taken totally by surprise. One minute they were having a good time, with not a care in the world, expecting the hostages to be delivered, the next minute they looked up from the river to see the entire English army massing opposite them on top of a small hill.

History often neglects to record the important things that people say, especially when under pressure. For instance, despite many theories we do not know the precise words of General Custer when he saw the Indians. We do not know the words of the captain of the Titanic when he saw the iceberg, and we do not know the words that Harald Hardrada said when he saw the English army, but you can bet it wasn't printable. Which is probably why it's never been printed and in consequence has been lost to posterity.

Being a good egg, prior to the start of the battle Harold rode out in front of his troops to speak with the Norwegian King and his brother Tostig. In an attempt to put off the promised bloodshed he offered his brother his old Earldom back. Tostig then asked what King Hardrada would receive for his troubles and after looking the large Norwegian up and down Harold answered "Seven feet of English earth!" The English troops that were within earshot fell about laughing at this joke, but it must have lost something in translation because when Tostig told Hardrada he didn't seem to get it, and rallied his troops into battle order.

The Vikings, thinking they were having a day off, were without their armour which, along with a third of their troops, they had left behind with their ships back at Riccall. They sent a runner back to get the reinforcements and tried to buy time by running across a small bridge to the opposite side of the river.

To guard the bridge they left one huge, hairy arsed Viking berserk armed with his axe. This Viking stood in the middle of the bridge which was so narrow that his attackers could only approach him one at a time and one at a time Harold's fighters took him on. To the shouts and yells of the Viking army this warrior swung his axe and an English head would sail from its English shoulders leaving a headless twitching body writhing on the bridge.

Twenty four bodiless heads were bobbing down the river before Harold decided to have a go himself. Afraid of him being the twenty fifth victim one of his commanders ran upstream and found a small boat. Lying in the bottom of this boat he allowed it to drift downstream until it floated under the bridge.

With an accuracy that belies the fact he was in a moving boat, he leapt to his feet and rammed his spear up through the bridge, and straight up the backside of the surprised Viking warrior. Thus creating the immortal saying made even more famous by Corporal Jones in that wonderful and much repeated television programme Dad's Army, "They don't like it up 'em!"

With the bridge now open Harold's army raced across and soon the two armies were locked in battle. The course of the battle went one way and then another but such was the fury unleashed by Harold's warriors that they eventually began to "win the day". Which is a very nice use of words used by writers of historical books to disguise the fact that axes inflicted horrendous wounds and pretty soon the English were knee deep in gore and bits and pieces of dead Vikings.

Eventually the Viking force was routed. Some tried to flee back to their ships but the English chased them and cut them down in a killing field that stretched for over nine miles. So many Vikings were killed that out of the three hundred ships there were only enough men left to sail twenty four back to Norway.

The battlefield site can still be seen at Stamford Bridge behind a corn mill that has been converted to a restaurant. If you stand up river, half close your eyes, ignore the smell of fish and chips and pretend that the caravan park doesn't exist you can almost imagine the scene that day. The actual battle is commemorated by a stone and plaque at the entrance to the Corn Mill whilst the local pub is named after the Viking axe man. Unfortunately the brewery, Sam Smiths, chose to name the pub "The Swordsman", complete with a pub sign showing a Viking berserk swinging a sword around his head. Then again they probably named it like that to help trade. I mean would you go frequent a pub that was called "The Mad Axeman"?

The victorious English army returned to York where they celebrated their victory by getting drunk and falling over a lot (a form of relaxation still enjoyed by many York people today). It is believed that the actual place where the victorious King Harold was celebrating his victory was a small inn on the river side, chosen by him because of their all day breakfasts which were famous throughout the land. It was stated in the Anglo Saxon chronicles that -

> *"The King and his thiegns and his housecarls were at their relaxations. Many were the sausages and eggs that were consumed, many were the bacon rolls and baked beans and the crispy chippies. Many also were the cups and horns that passed their lips that day, and merry were the celebrations.*
>
> *Jesters jested, tumblers tumbled, harpers harped, and many were the numbers of*

acoustic singer songwriters that lay passed out behind the bar."

In the middle of these festivities terrible news reached York when that morning's copy of the "Saxon Chronicle and Daily Herald" popped through the letter box. The lead story was not of the Battle of Stamford Bridge. Instead Harold read that William and the Normans had landed for the next round of the Intercity Battle of the Bands Competition, to be held the following week at Hastings. It is recorded that as he read the fearful news Harold murmured his immortal words -

"Oh bugger me! Now we're in for it!"

He left the city the following morning never to return, meeting his death a couple of weeks later in Hastings at the hands of William's victorious Norman Army. The Normans, despitc having a natural cruel streak in them, did not have the imagination of the Saxons and only hacked Harold's body to pieces. Then in the aftermath of battle, feeling guilty about it, they had to find and collect them all and put them back together again so Harold could be buried on the nearby cliff tops, ironically looking across the channel, which was the Normans idea of a joke. Back in York the owners of the small inns and cafe bars quietly changed their menu to allow for the more exotic tastes of the French. Bread buns became croissants, bacon was replaced by L'Escargo, lard was replaced by L'Margarine, spam was replaced by Pate, and beef was replaced by horse meat. Worst of all the Norman age heralded the return of the wine bar.

CHAPTER FIVE

NORMAN YORK.

William's Coronation at Westminster Abbey didn't delight everyone in Saxon England. For two years he kept himself busy subjugating the South and West, ignoring the North but unfortunately the Northumbrians wouldn't let things well alone. In 1068, under Earl Cospatric they revolted and for the first time William's attention was drawn to the North. He decided to pay them a visit and, as he travelled up the country, he stopped off in the Midlands and built castles in Warwick and Nottingham, then he entered Yorkshire.

The sight of the Norman army marching up the A64 was enough to put anyone off, and it did! The leaders of the revolt took to their heels and ran off in the opposite direction, ending up in Scotland, whilst the more sensible occupants of York met William at the city entrance and handed him the keys to the city. However William didn't become the ruler he was by trusting the people he had conquered and, before he left the city, he built a motte and bailey castle on the west bank of the Ouse and garrisoned it with five hundred men. He gave the command of this garrison to one of his knights, William Malet, who had fought with him at Hastings. He gave the responsibility of looking after all of Yorkshire to another of his knights, Robert FitzRichard, also for services rendered.

Bearing in mind the fact that York was still principally a Danish town and owed more allegiance to Scandinavia than it did to London, the occupants were not too happy about this new garrison overlooking their town. Especially as at the end of every week on pay day, the Normans rode out and collected taxes from anyone they came across, usually at sword point thus redefining the notion of direct taxation.

It was only a matter of time before Northumbria was up in arms again and in 1068, an army from Durham rebelled and killed their Norman overlord. Not wanting to feel left out Yorkshire also rebelled, and killed Robert FitzRichard. Earl Cospatric who had returned from Scotland just for the occasion, laid siege to the garrison.

William turned back from London and attacked the city and the Northumbrian army. Throughout York there was fierce hand to hand fighting, which the Normans won hands down. When they made sure that there were no more Northumbrians left the Normans set about ransacking and plundering the city. They took everything that wasn't nailed down, and then came back again for the nails.

Even worse, William decided that the townspeople of York hadn't learnt their lesson, and built a second fortified castle on the opposite side of the river, where Clifford's Tower stands today. Command of this castle was given to another of William's Hastings veterans, William FitzOsbern.

Having rebelled against the Normans and their one castle, and been hammered out of sight you would think that the Northumbrian people would have learnt their lesson, but no, stupidity not only ran in the family, occasionally it galloped. In the spring of 1069 a large Northumbrian army gathered north of the city but FitzOsbern and his garrison rallied out of his castle and defeated them. It was now three - nil in favour of the Normans and FitzOsbern could be forgiven for thinking that he had won game set and match. He returned to his castle, put his feet up and was just about to send his tax collectors out again when someone looked out of the window and saw a huge Danish Army heading towards the town. This army had sailed up the Humber, disembarked and joined up with what was left of Cospatric's army and attacked the town without even bothering to knock on the gate.

It is always the case that, just when you think things can't get any worse, they usually do. In order to stop the Danish army sheltering in the town and sneaking up to the castle, some bright Norman lad had the idea of setting fire to the surrounding houses. Unfortunately the wind changed at the critical moment and the flames swept through the town destroying the Minster, the Minster Library, and many other buildings. The Danish Army took advantage of the confusion and attacked the garrison killing every Norman in sight, however their victory was hollow to say the least. By the time they finished fighting the fire had died down and the city was devastated and indefensible. The Danes took everything that the Normans had left behind and went off back to their boats.

This was the greatest defeat the Normans ever experienced in England and to say that William was pissed off is to give new meaning to the expression. He was annoyed, antagonized, choleric, displeased, enraged, exasperated, incensed, indignant, infuriated, irascible, irate, ireful, irritated, out-raged, piqued, raging, riled, and splenetic, all at the same time. When his close friends finally got him down from the ceiling he gathered his army and marched North once again. He got to Castleford where he made a deal with the Danes and paid them an awful lot of money to go away. Then he marched on York. There was no opposition. He re-took what was left of the city, set about re-building his castles, and then set about teaching the Yorkshire Northumbrians a lesson they wouldn't forget.

Unfortunately by the time he had finished teaching this lesson there was hardly anyone left alive to remember it. Throughout the winter of 1069-70 William swept through Yorkshire burning and killing everything it was possible to burn or kill.

As we mentioned earlier, historians have devised a number of weasel words that cover up the actual awful truth of what really happened. The words they use for this devastation, this scorched earth policy, is the phrase "The Harrying of the North." In my dictionary the word *"Harry" means 1. to harass; worry. 2. to ravage (a town etc.), esp. in war.* It does not mean killing everything that moved and burning to ashes everything that didn't. William destroyed houses, farms, barns, crops and farm implements. He destroyed pubs, shops, churches, village halls and bus stops. He killed men, women, children, babies, horses, cattle, sheep, chickens, kittens, puppy dogs and bunny rabbits. It is estimated that over 100,000 people died as a result of his actions, and for years afterwards the land between York and Durham was a deserted wasteland. It is no wonder that William's autobiography was called "The Domesday Book"!

Having lived through their town being attacked and ravaged by Northumbrians from Durham, Vikings from Norway, Scots from

Glasgow, Danes from Denmark, and having seen it almost burnt to a frazzle, the few surviving citizens of York finally threw in the towel when they saw the Normans from France sitting in their brand new garrison at small white tables under umbrellas, eating onion soup and barbecuing their lamb. They knew in their heart of hearts that Saxon England had disappeared forever, and before long they would all be members of the EC. From this day on the English have had to put up with things like the Euro Tunnel and Le Shuttle, Euro Disney, croissants, brie, pate, wine bars and the dreaded ECU, a mythical beast that lives deep in a cave in Brussels.

The country settled down under their new rulers with the exception of the men of East Anglia. In 1070, under an English Lord called Hereward The Wake, the Saxon inventor of the alarm clock, they rebelled. However despite hiding in the marshes of the Fens the Normans, who had been issued with Wellington boots, laid siege to the rebels and soon all English resistance was wiped out.

Having destroyed York the Normans set about building it up again but, still being a bit wary, they started off by re-building their castle first . On an earthen mound they built a large wooden tower whilst below, on an area of land that now comprises the area occupied by The Castle Museum, they built the lower bailey, a wooden stockade that housed barracks, guardrooms, kitchens, a chapel, a bistro, a pissoire, and other structures used for purposes that only the Normans knew.

In 1069 William appointed Thomas of Bayeux, tapestry maker extraodinaire, as Archbishop of York. Thomas arrived in the city to find only a burnt out shell of a building. He set to, rolled his sleeves up and began the re-building operations. He then established a governing body of thirty six canons ruled over by a Dean, a Precentor, Chancellor and Treasurer, and told them to get on with things.

One of the most drastic alterations the Normans made to the city was the damming of the River Foss. This dam created a huge lake that covered over 150 acres of land to the east of the city and was given the name of "The Kings Fish Pond", an early example of the use of Saxon irony. Whilst this new urban improvement was good for the Normans, even providing a moat around their fine new castle, it was a pain in the arse for the native York residents.

Firstly it flooded a number of houses and mills and caused rising damp in the rest of the houses. Secondly it provided the city a staple diet of fish, for several hundred years! Whilst the Normans sat in their castle on the hill reading old copies of Le Monde and Paris Match and eating spit roast lamb, what was left of the English residents ate fish. It was fish for breakfast, lunch, and dinner. It was fish Monday, Tuesday, Wednesday, Thursday, Friday, Saturday and, just for a change, on Sunday, more bloody fish. Archaeologists working in York have actually found the skeletal remains of people from this period and made the shattering discovery that some of them ate so much fish that they had actually started to grow scales, gills and fins.

A road from the Norman castle, called surprisingly enough Castlegate, led straight to the centre of the burnt out city where the remains of Danish King's palaces, the Minster and numerous other house and shops lay blackened and burnt out. An indication of this devastation can be found in various documentation. During the reign of Edward the Confessor the town had around two thousand occupied houses. In 1086 only one thousand five hundred remained of which five hundred were empty burnt out shells and another four hundred just lay empty. Someone who must have been given a pocket calculator for Christmas worked out that the population before 1066 was around eight to nine thousand, and twenty years later was less than half that number. It must have been a very bad time for the town's estate agents.

The Normans divided the town into areas called wards. The new Archbishop got the area around the Minster called "the Liberty of St. Peter", whilst the largest landowner, after William himself, was William's half brother, the Count of Mortain. The city itself was governed from the castle by a person with the title of King's Sheriff. He was responsible to the King for keeping law and order, and for the collection of taxes, a position that must have made him a really popular bloke with what remained of the townspeople. It does explain why most of the time he stayed inside the castle and only came out at special occasions, usually guarded by a gang of heavily armed Norman troops.

CHAPTER SIX

THE EARLY MIDDLE AGES.

The period of English history from 1066 to the 1400's is called the Middle Ages. This is because history was invented in the 20th century and the period in question falls approximately in the middle of the period from Roman conquest to the present day. Which is OK for us living at the present time but is surely going to confuse historians in the next thousand years. It's interesting to speculate whether in the year 2999 they will rename the period the Quarter Ages! There again, there could be a lot more interesting things to speculate about!

Anyway, as the Middle Ages lasted so long, and so much happened during them, and in the belief that history can only be handled in small digestible chunks, historians have decided to sub-divide the Middle Ages into two periods called oddly enough The Early Middle Ages and The Late Middle Ages. There are no prizes for guessing which came first!

In 1071 William gave another of his mates a job and promoted Lanfranc to the position of Archbishop of Canterbury. Lanfranc was Italian and, as well as being a churchman, was also well versed in civil law. Soon he organised the English Church establishing a structure that would remain until Henry VIII came along and cheerfully dismantled it. Some of Lanfranc's many achievements were the re-establishment of the monasteries, monastic schools and ecclesiastical courts of law - things that had their effect up and down the land, but especially in York where the building of religious structures helped to re-establish the York building industry.

Again when you're looking in one direction, trouble usually appears behind you. As soon as William gained the upper hand trouble flared up in France and William returned to the continent where he spent the next few years battling and keeping Normandy free from the grabbing hands of ambitious French barons and Kings.

In 1087 war broke out between William and King Philip I of France. In July William had seized the French town of Mantes and, true to Norman tradition, burnt it to the ground. Unfortunately his new horse wasn't used to huge flames roaring through the air and the smell of singed horsehair. It reared, throwing William onto the hard French ground. The resulting fall gave him a nasty bump on the head from which he never recovered and he died on 9th September at Rouen.

Three weeks later William's empire was divided up between his two eldest sons. The eldest son Robert was made Duke of Normandy whilst the second son William Rufus was crowned William II, King of England. Together they conspired to prevent William's third son Henry from getting his hands on anything.

This state of affairs upset a lot of Normans who had sworn loyalty to one or other of the two brothers but owned property in both England and Normandy and now didn't know which one to serve. Some thought that it would be the better option to get rid of William Rufus and make Robert King, whilst the rest thought they were better off with Rufus and there were rebellions in 1088 and again in 1095. But William was a better soldier and had a bigger treasure chest, two considerations which soon persuaded the barons and lords to join with him and Robert was left isolated in Normandy.

However the English, whether Norman or Saxon, lord or baron, soon got fed up to the back teeth of William Rufus. It is said that he had lax morals, bled the church dry of its funds, and made his greedy financial advisor Flambard the Archbishop of Durham. What was worse was that he squandered the tax money on living a decadent lifestyle. For William II it was party, party all the time, and if such things as sex and drugs and rock 'n roll had been around he would have had a lifestyle similar to the popular singing icon Ozzy Osborne.

William Rufus' great love was hunting and he introduced Draconian laws in the King's forests to prevent anyone else from doing it. Great expanses of England's forests were set aside as Royal Hunting lands where the deer and wild boar were only allowed to be killed by the king, whilst barons and abbots were allowed to hunt lesser game such as rabbits, hare and fox. The lower classes were only allowed to hunt such animals as hedgehogs, mice, voles and weasels.

After thirteen years of misrule William had become so unpopular that no one was surprised when one day whilst out hunting he was shot in the chest by a bolt, not from the blue, but from a crossbow. To this day who actually did the deed is a mystery that would have puzzled even Brother Cadfael, the great medieval detective monk.

Some claim that the dirty deed was done by a French noble called Walter Tirel who just happened to be the only person out hunting with William when he got the crossbow bolt in the chest, especially as the two men had argued the night before. Also Tirel didn't do his cause any good when, as the King lay dying, he jumped on his horse and legged it in the opposite direction. However others claim the assassin was William's younger brother Henry, who just happened to be hunting in the same forest at the same time. It was also suspicious that instead of going to his dying brother's aid, or even chasing the fleeing Tirel, Henry jumped on his horse, galloped to Winchester, and seized the royal treasury. Thus carrying on the tradition of the "Golden Rule". He had the gold so he got to rule!

Henry I took over the Kingdom and tried to establish some essence of stability, despite having to fight rebellious barons, and having a protracted argument with the church. His position made him cautious to the point of paranoia. He frequently changed his servants, had armed guards at every doorway, had his sword hanging at the side of his bed which every night he moved around his chamber. But Henry's greatest problem was that of succession. Despite being a prolific father and having twenty two children, only two of them were actually born to his wife. His son Prince William was drowned when his ship, manned by a crew of drunken sailors, hit the rocks off the Normandy coast and sank, which only left his daughter Mathilda as a direct Norman descendent. However, as Mathilda had married a European Emperor called Henry V and had not been to England since she was eight years old, various factions promoted a series of other potential royal heirs. Some barons supported Duke Robert, others supported his son William Clito. Yet another faction supported Stephen of Bois, a son of William the Conqueror's daughter. Complicated? You bet!

However tangles sometimes do have a habit of sorting themselves out. Henry ruled for another fifteen years during which William Clito, Duke Robert, and Emperor Henry V all died. Mathilda remarried one Geoffrey of Anjou and promptly in 1133, gave birth to a son, also called Henry. At this stage it's worth a thought to ponder that, if the ruling classes of the day had more imagination and called their sons by different names, history would be a lot less confusing.

Henry I travelled to France to try to sort the issue out, but when he got there it turned out that Mathilda didn't have the required gentility to rule. She ate with her elbows on the table, belched loudly after every meal and frequently let off wind without excusing herself or without even trying to pass the blame onto anyone else. As a result Stephen became favourite for the job.

Henry I died in December 1133 from eating a plateful of eels. This was deemed his own fault as his doctor had warned him to stay away from them. Eels are a dodgy sort of food at the best of time - even Londoners only eat them after they have been first been boiled for three weeks, and then only after they have been first immersed in something that looks and tastes like KY Jelly.

Henry's body was still warm when Stephen caught the first available ferry across the channel and grabbed the English throne for himself. Within a month he was crowned King of England, but understandably enough, this action annoyed Mathilda and her supporters so much that for the next nineteen years the country was divided. Civil war broke out, valuables were buried, swords were sharpened, spears re-pointed, and armies marched all over the place. They occasionally bumped into one another, fought a bit, and then marched off again.

Stephen was captured and, for some years, held prisoner, then he escaped. Then the tables turned. Mathilda was nearly captured, escaping from a besieged Oxford castle across the frozen river. Very quickly the country sank into total anarchy. The Crown had been reduced to poverty, and the bodies of many influential lords and barons were left rotting on various battlefields. The only law was that administered by different barons, who themselves were no better than a gang of mobsters. In short it was a situation similar to gangland New York, as depicted by the very fine musical play West Side Story, only for Sharks and Jets read Stephen and Mathilda. Eventually someone saw fit to bang their heads together and, in 1153, a truce was drawn up on the understanding that on Stephen's death the crown would pass to Mathilda's son, yet another Henry!

Stephen died eleven months later and, at the age of twenty one, Henry Plantagenet copped for the Kingdom of England. Despite being considered a bit young for the job Henry II had vast practical experience. On the death of his mother and father he had become Lord of Normandy, Anjou, Maine and Touraine. When he was nineteen he married Eleanor of Aquataine who was eleven years his elder and who entered into the marriage with a string of lovers in tow. She had already been married once before, to the King of France, but the marriage had been annulled because she could not bear him children. However it must have been the French king that fired blanks because, as Henry's wife she gave birth to five sons and three girls.

By the time the pair of them got married and Henry crowned King of England between them they owned an area of land that stretched from the Cheviot Hills to the Pyrenees. Not bad for such a young couple! Governing such an area wasn't easy and, as half his time was spent in France, Henry created a judicial and administrative system that would work very happily without him. This system involved the creation of travelling Kings Justices who were not only responsible for sorting out legal problems but also collected taxes. Henry also spiked the power of the Barons by establishing something called common law, created a jury system, and laid the law down banning the fortification of castles without his permission. He also dictated the type of weapons that could be carried by different ranks of his subjects. Barons and Lords could have great two handed swords, shields and lances. Lesser ranks could have smaller swords and bows and arrows, farmers could have scythes and pointed sticks and the commoners could have blunt sticks and catapults. Beggars, tramps and other people at the bottom of the food chain were allowed to throw small stones.

All these major events happened down south, and whilst the rest of the country was awash with various argumentative and warring factions York simply got on with the job of re-building itself. A number of churches were constructed, the walls of the city were re-fortified with wooden palisades. The Minster was re-built, as were a number of churches and other religious structures and slowly the City began to raise phoenix like out of the ashes.

In 1086 Count Alan of Brittany had given St. Olav's Church and four acres of land to some Benedictine monks on which they began to build an abbey. In his time, prior to the crossbow incident, William Rufus enlarged this area and granted the monks a charter establishing St. Mary's Abbey. Everything was going splendidly until 1137 when, forgetting their ineptitude with fire, a Norman soldier accidentally dropped a lighted match onto a pile of straw and once again the City burnt to the ground.

Once the smoke had cleared away everyone sighed, rolled their sleeves up and began to rebuild the city once again. In our present time we are used to building work being a fast track sort of operation. Companies such as Tay Homes, Barratts and Persimmons have got the practice down to a fine art. Indeed these days you can go for a week's holiday and when you get back a brand new housing complex has been erected in your back garden. But building in the Middle Ages took far longer. Some critics, embittered by modern building trends, might be tempted to say that in those days they built to last.

Henry II visited York at least three times. Typically, whenever royalty visit a city, improvements that the people have been demanding for years suddenly and miraculously happen. Just as today, if ever a town centre needs a coat of paint, the first thing to do is to invite Royalty for a visit. Each time Henry II visited York he was asked to repair York Castle. In his visit of 1172 he paid £15 to repair the wooden tower and in 1175 he carried out more repairs and refurbishments.

However in those days they didn't really build to last, it was a myth. When King Henry III spent his Christmas holidays at residence in York Castle in 1228 dinner had just reached the stage when the brandy on the Christmas pudding was lit, there was a mighty gust of wind and the castle's main gate and wooden tower fell over. Annoyed by the fact that his pudding had got cold whilst he went outside to see what the commotion was all about, Henry left the castle as it was and allowed the building to deteriorate.

In 1244 a threat of war with Scotland brought the King back to York. He spent a thoroughly miserable night at the Castle due to the fact that one of the walls to his bedroom was missing. That was bad enough, but as in today's society, the presence of royalty creates a natural curiosity in all manner of people. All night a long procession of towns people passed by the hole in the wall to openly gawp on his recumbent figure. The following morning he got up and ordered the castle to be rebuilt of stone.

Records state that this building work was carried out by one Anthony D'Embo, a builder and player of the huppity horn, a medieval wind instrument. To this day his name can be found carved into a stone hidden deep in the cellars behind the back of the Castle Museum. Anthony D'Embo himself was a well known York personality. As well as being a successful builder he played popular music with a group of travelling musicians known as "Ye Goosefoot Brothers". For some years this musical group played in various York taverns and at local celebrations and festivities. They were most famous however for their annual riotous performance on the eve of the celebration of St. John of the Black Bagge, which sometimes lasted well into the following Stranglers Tuesday, providing the ale held out.

As the weeks, months and years flashed by building work continued throughout the City. St. Mary's Abbey was eventually completed sometime from 1270 onwards. When it was finished it was a magnificent building 350 feet long with an aisled nave and choir, transepts and a central tower complete with spire.

Other religious houses built around this period were the Holy Trinity Priory on Micklegate, a house of Augustinian Friars on the side of the River Ouse near to where the Guildhall now stands, a Franciscan priory near to the Castle, a Dominican priory near to Toft Green, and a Carmelite House to the east of the city by the River Foss.

These were just the more popular religious establishments. Other less well known ones also thrived inside the city. One of these was the small but curious order of Carmelite Nuns who built a small wooden hut near Lendal and who followed the teachings of St. Kimberly of the High Jump. This Lesser Saint was meant to have worked with St. Patrick in the foundation of early Irish monasteries, only she was not as successful as he was in the handling of snakes. Whilst St. Patrick only had to point at a snake and it would slither into the nearest river or sea, and emigrate by swimming across to America, St. Kimberly would point and the snakes would grin and slither towards her. This state of affairs led to the unfortunate Saint often having to gather up her skirts and leap into the air to avoid their nasty teeth and fangs. The unfortunate woman would then have to remain leaping and jumping until either the snake went away or she was rescued by St. Patrick.

In-line with her teachings and to commemorate her life and work, every hour on the hour, her small but dedicated band of followers would lift their skirts and leap into the air, shrieking all the while. This observance was fine as long as it was confined inside their own small abbey, however on the streets of medieval York it was another thing. Despite the advantage of being able to accurately tell the time by them, the towns citizens soon became fed up of leaping, shrieking nuns everywhere and claimed they caused a public disturbance.

Eventually, after a particularly nasty incident that occurred in 1182 involving a leaping nun, a market trader and a large cauliflower, a bye-law was passed forbidding the nuns to jump "within three lamb's tails of the city walls". As they held a hundred years lease on their building the order had to abandon their following of St. Kimberly and instead took up the teachings of "St. Mungo the Quiet and Placid" and were never heard of again.

It seemed during this period that most building work was directed towards the erection of religious structures. Around this time there were seventeen hospitals and almshouses built, the major one being St. Leonard's. This hospital was situated near to St. Mary's Abbey and with a hundred and fifty beds was the largest hospital in England. It was originally built before the fire of 1137 and named St. Peter's but when it was rebuilt its name changed to St. Leonard's. The hospital was famous throughout the land for treating the poor and giving them free Sunday lunches.

It is believed that it was from their kitchens that the first Yorkshire pudding was concocted. This invention came about because, as every true Yorkshireman and woman knows, large dollops of good Yorkshire Pudding is not only cheap and nourishing, but it is very filling. It was discovered by the monks that if they served this pudding before they served up the meat and two veg, the poor couldn't eat as much of the more expensive food. As it was served with great dollops of gravy the poor didn't mind, especially as it made a welcome change from bloody fish every day.

In 1143 William FitzHerbert, a great grandson of William the Conqueror, and nephew of King Stephen, was made Archbishop of York, proving that nepotism was not dead but was very much alive, even down to the third generation. Despite his influential connections and his highly exalted position Archbishop William was a very popular figure in the city, a fact that led to one of York's most bizarre accidents.

In 1154 William returned to the city from a visit to the seaside and the population were so pleased to see him back home safely that they gathered to welcome him on the wooden Ouse Bridge. It seems that the Archbishop, instead of walking along the middle of the road, appeared on the river bank and waved to his gathered fans. In response to this wave the people on the bridge all rushed to one side to wave back to him and the weight of the crowd caused the ancient structure to overbalance. The bridge collapsed into the river and all the people fell into the water. The irony of the fact is that, according to a nearby onlooker, Archbishop William wasn't waving, he was pointing and saying to the bloke next to him, "Look at that daft lot over there. If they're not careful they'll be off that bloody bridge!"

The collapsed remains of the wooden bridge were eventually replaced by one of stone which, in the thirteenth century was lined with buildings. It housed the York Council Chamber, the Mayor's Parlour, a prison, a hospital, a chapel, and twenty houses with a parade of shops on each side. Indeed when a resident of the city walked across the bridge it was as if he was just walking along a normal street. In those days there were no pretty views of the river, no lamp posts and hanging flower baskets, just buildings, buildings and more buildings.

The Norman's had strengthened the city's defence by building wooden palisades on top of the existing earthen banks, which in turn were replaced around 1250 by stone battlements, with the exception of the area around the Kings Fish Pond. This area of duck, otter and fish infested water was guarded by two new towers, Layerthorpe Postern and Red Tower. New gates and entrances to the city were constructed, but for some reason they were called "bars". Over the years this misnomer has proved very confusing to American tourists who, when they are at home, all drink in bars and are unfamiliar with the concept of the English pub. Hence a common sight at Micklegate, Monkgate, Bootham and Walmgate, is to find queues of bemused Americans trying to find somewhere to buy a bottle of Budweiser whilst they walk straight past such wonderful places as The Three Tuns, The Bonding Warehouse, The Hansom Cab, and The Cross Keys, oblivious of the alcoholic delights they contain.

Once the walls and bars had been constructed the city must have looked pretty impressive and impregnable, and it is no great surprise to discover that they looked so sturdy that no one bothered to attack them for the next four hundred years or so. Oddly enough when they were put to the test, in 1644 during the siege of York, they did not prove very effective, but there again, that's ornamental walling for you!

CHAPTER SEVEN

THE LATE MIDDLE AGES.

When Edward I ascended to the throne of England in 1272 the first thing he did was to fall out with Llywelyn ap Gruffydd the leader of the Welsh. In 1282 Llywelyn persuaded the Welsh to revolt and in retaliation, Edward marched his army into Wales. Eight months later Llywelyn was killed and Edward, determined that the Welsh would never rise again, spent the next 21 years building a series of castles all over the Welsh countryside.

Having finally subdued the Welsh, Edward then turned his attention to the Scots who in 1295 had upset him by supporting the French. The following year Edward attacked Scotland. By August he had sacked Berwick, defeated a Scots army and marched on to Elgin, on his way pinching a stone scone which he promptly hid under his chair in Westminster Abbey.

In 1296 Edward joined an alliance with the Count of Flanders against France but whilst he was looking the other way a Scot named William Wallace led an uprising in Scotland. This rebellion defeated an English army at Stirling Bridge and travelled south attacking Northumberland and Cumberland. In 1298 Edward returned to England and moved his court to York, which he figured was a good place to fight the Scots from, and York Castle got another lick of paint.

By July Edward had invaded Scotland, beating William Wallace at the Battle of Falkirk. After the battle Wallace fled from Scotland and Edward returned south, but, as soon as his back was turned, the Scots attacked and re-captured Stirling Castle. Throughout the summer of 1300 Edward led a series of unsuccessful campaigns in Scotland before agreeing to a truce in October. Mind you it seems that the truce was only agreed upon because the English didn't like fighting in the Scottish winters because in the summer of 1301 Edward was back again, this time advancing into the country from Berwick whilst his son, Prince Edward attacked from Carlisle. This pincer attack brought all Scotland south of the River Forth under their rule and they administered it from their northern capital at York.

That winter Edward again agreed to a truce, which lasted until the summer of 1303 when he began yet another campaign. He wintered in Dunfermline Abbey and, in March 1304, the Scottish Barons finally submitted to him. That is all the Barons with the exception of William Wallace who had come back to Scotland and ensconced himself once again in Stirling Castle. In April Edward besieged Stirling Castle and in May the Scots surrendered. The following year William Wallace was captured, was tried and executed in an extremely nasty way. He was hanged, drawn and quartered, with bits of his body being placed in different parts of the country.

This event was recently commemorated by the Hollywood blockbuster "Braveheart" starring the actor Mel Gibson. Sadly it seems that when it comes to writing about history Britain is good at producing books, but if you want to attract any funding to make a half decent movie about it you have to go to America, get the interest of a California based film company, who then bring in an Australian film actor, and who end up filming most of the scenes in Ireland!

Unfortunately for Edward, the Scots now found themselves a bloke called Robert The Bruce who could handle himself pretty well. It seems that he could also handle a battle axe just as well. As his "starter for ten" Bruce murdered his rival to the Scottish throne, John Comyn, re-took Dumfries and crowned himself King of Scotland. Edward attacked Scotland once again, Bruce was defeated and hid for a few months in a cave with only a large black spider for company. The spider eventually persuaded Robert to have another go and he returned, beat an English army, and began to grab back all the land that Edward had captured.

All this coming and going, winning and losing was too much for Edward and in 1307, he died of frustration at Burgh-upon-Sands, leading his army across the Scottish Borders in what he rightly, but somewhat ironically, called his last great campaign.

Edward was succeeded by his son Edward II who also spent most of his energies fighting the Scots, only less successfully. In 1314 he and an army of around twenty thousand men managed to get themselves totally routed by Robert The Bruce at Bannockburn. Edward escaped but left behind him a defeated army, many of his knights, and the Privy Seal of England. Bruce meanwhile established himself King of an independent Scotland and revived his unusual hobby of spider watching.

Losing Scotland made Edward very unpopular with the English lords, barons, knights and gentlefolk. Mind you, he wasn't very popular to begin with. During his reign he, as history books so quaintly say, "Lavished his attention on a court favourite". This is "historian speak" for saying that the guy was gay. Nowadays in this more enlightened age, society looks upon homosexuality more sympathetically, but in the Middle Ages it would be magnanimous to say that it was frowned upon. It was abominated, despised, abhorred, and detested, especially if the person in question was the heir to throne. The object of Edward's attentions was a young effeminate French knight called Peirs Gaveston and, even before Edward was crowned, the scandal got so bad that his father Edward I banished the French knight from the heterosexual English court.

To dispel any doubts about his sexuality, in 1308 Edward married a woman called Isabella but the first thing he did when he became King was to bring Gaveston back to the court and promote him to Earl of Cornwall. It was no surprise that the English Lords objected and, in 1308, they forced Edward to banish him once again, which he did, but only for a year. The pair were soon reunited and spent a cosy Christmas together at Windsor. Soon the corridors of power were once again smelling of Eau de Cologne and Gaveston was promoted to the position of Kings Lieutenant in Ireland.

For many English lords that would have been the straw that broke the camel's back, if they had known what a camel looked like. As it was, civil war broke out. To avoid the angry lords and barons Edward fled to York Castle and re-fortified the building by constructing a new outer ditch and a wooden palisade. He also built a moat that divided the stone keep from the rest of the castle, and gave it a new coat of paint.

Eventually due to political pressure, Edward was forced to create the Lords Ordainers, a council of nobles led by his cousin Thomas, Earl of Lancaster, whose job was to oversee the government of England. Their first act was to banish Gaveston once again. Off he went only to get a cheap day return to the continent and be back by tea. The council tried to get rid of him once again and offered him a safe passage back to France. Gaveston agreed, but unfortunately as he was being taken to the ferry he was captured by the Earl of Warwick, a well known homophobic, who promptly led Gaveston through the streets of Warwick to somewhere called Blacklow Hill where he had him executed.

That same month Bruce, bored with watching spiders, invaded England as far south as Durham, and the following year captured Perth, Roxburgh, Edinburgh and the Isle of Man. Once again Edward invaded Scotland, but got thrashed at Bannockburn and fled back south to York followed by a victorious rampaging Scots army who raided as far south as Richmond before returning home. Then they turned their attention towards Ireland. Over the next four years Bruce and his brother Edward fought and took Ireland, but in 1315 they lost the Irish support and had to abandon their siege of Dublin. Roger Mortimer was made Justicart of Ireland and beat the Scots back north. Fed up of the reception they received by the Irish they came home and in 1318 they attacked England once again, this time getting as far south as Ripon. Once again Edward was forced to march north and, in 1319, again using York as his base, he attacked Berwick.

Meanwhile a Scottish raiding party headed for York in an attempt to capture the court and Queen Isabella. The court fled south leaving the Mayor of York, one Nicholas Fleming, to lead an army to attack the Scots at Myton-In-Swale. They were defeated, Fleming was killed and the victorious Scots marched further south towards Pontefract.

If facing attacks from the Scots wasn't bad enough Edward also faced argumentative English Lords led by the Earl of Lancaster. Edward challenged him to a bit of a scrap, defeated and executed him at the Battle of Boroughbridge. Then, flushed with success and having not learnt his lesson, the King chose to "lavish his affections on another court favourite", one Hugh Le Despenser. Once again the proverbial stuff hit the proverbial fan. Fed up with the bedroom antics of her AC/DC husband Queen Isabella took herself off in a huff to France on the pretext of a trade mission, promptly fell in love with someone called Mortimer and refused to come home.

However she wasn't a woman who forgave and forgot easily. Determined to give her husband a lesson he wouldn't forget she returned, not only bringing her lover with her, but also bringing a bloody great army that as soon as it landed overran the country. Edward was captured, imprisoned in Berkeley Castle and forced to abdicate in favour of his son Edward III who was crowned 1st February 1327. In September of the same year Edward II was murdered. Many history books say that no one knows how this murder was committed, only that it was done in such a way as to cause maximum agony whilst leaving no mark on the royal body. This leads the reader to horrific speculations involving a hollow horn and a red hot poker. The very thought of which makes one wince so much that your eyes water. Edward's certainly did!

Three years after Edward II rebuilt York Castle in stone a disturbing discovery was made. The castle was slowly sinking. The frequent flooding of both the Foss and the Ouse had softened the ground and it could no longer support the weight of the stone building. The foundations slipped and the walls of the castle began to crack and fall over. This was around the time the King had beaten Lancaster at the Battle of Boroughbridge which wasn't a cheap affair and in consequence he had no money left to pay for refurbishments. It was only in 1326 that some money was found to erect buttresses to hold the building up, but even then the amount raised wasn't enough to buttress the keep as well. Instead of refurbishments the building only got a new name due to Edward II hanging a bloke called Robert de Clifford in chains from the top and leaving him there to die.

Today, if a property owner wants to get a listed building demolished, all they have to do is to leave it alone and let it fall down by itself. It wasn't much different in the 14th century. York Castle had deteriorated even further and no one had bothered to lift a finger to help it. By 1360 it had cracked in two, most of the timber had been burnt for fuel, and someone had swiped the lead. The dungeon was useless because of flooding. It was so damp that even the rats wore water wings. Surveyors recommended that it should be pulled down and rebuilt from scratch but still nothing was done. Even Royal visitors to York refused to go near the place, preferring instead to stay at the nearby Holiday Inn.

When Edward came to York he brought with him a number of foreign mercenaries led by someone called John, Lord Beaumont of Hainault. For some reason, probably to do with the fact that the city had been under threat from foreign attackers for the last few hundred years, the citizens of York took exception to the arrival of more foreigners and fighting broke out.

John went home in 1328 but came back the next year bringing with him his niece Philippa, daughter of William Earl of Hainault, Holland and Zealand. Philippa was deemed a suitable match for Edward and the couple were duly married in York Minster. The event was celebrated in the City by a three week binge of jousting, revelling, feasting, dancing and generally everyone just getting totally pissed, still a favourite recreation of the York residents. However, as anyone who has ventured into York on a Saturday night knows, being in the city with a lot of pissed residents can be very dangerous, and in 1329 it was no exception, especially as there were no bouncers guarding the pub doorways then.

Once again hostilities broke out between the residents and the visitors from Hainault. Minor punch-ups occurred throughout the city but the residents of York really took exception when the foreigners set fire to one of the city's suburbs. A formal challenge was issued and the citizens met the foreigners in a pitched battle that raged throughout the city and ended up on the banks of the river where everyone managed to fall in. In the ensuing fracas 347 Hainaulters and 242 English were drowned.

Despite staying at the Holiday Inn every time he visited Edward wasn't very impressed with York. He said that the city was one of the most disgusting places in his kingdom. The streets were filled with butchers offal, uncollected garbage, nasty dead furry things and human waste. To alleviate the problem public loos were built on the castle moat and at the end of Ouse Bridge, however the excrement wasn't washed away down sewers and to waste water treatment plants, it just dropped through a round hole into the water and stayed there to fester, rot and create a very unhealthy stink.

In addition to the stink of human excrement the town was also full of animals. Dogs and cats skulked in the streets and alleyways. Chickens ran riot. Pigs ran up and down the streets, usually closely followed by irate owners in the vain hope of catching them before they ran anywhere near the street occupied by the butchers. Any animal that ventured within a few hundred yards of the butchers' street was never seen again. Regardless of its edibility or number of legs, it usually ended up as a joint of meat or, in the case of cats, rats, dogs and anything else a bit strange, in meat pies.

As well as the terrible stink and wading through offal the inhabitants of the city also had to put up with living in houses infested with rats, mice and lice. All in all the town was a far cry from the cosy picture of medieval England depicted on Christmas cards and souvenir place mats.

To be fair to York it wasn't really any different from any other major European city and it was these unsanitary conditions that led to the spread of the very nasty and cheerfully named disease called The Black Death which swept through Europe and arrived in England, hitting the North around 1349. As it was, the life expectancy of the average York citizen was only thirty eight years and the arrival of the Black Death created a severe downward trend in those statistics.

Having yet to develop a sense of irony, The Black Death was aptly named by the medieval folk. Its symptoms were not very nice. It started by glands swelling up to the size of grapefruit, then the entire body slowly turned black. The swellings then festered for four to five days before the unfortunate victim died.

Throughout England the disease took no prisoners. Over one thousand villages were wiped out. It is estimated that the Black Death killed one third of the country's population. Many rich people fled from the towns and lived in their country estates, locking their doors behind them and throwing things at anyone who tried to call. Of course the poor had to stay where they were and keep their fingers crossed, which was just about as effective as any other available medicine. London was so deserted that Edward III was forced to dissolve Parliament. Many people refused to travel and very little food reached towns, adding starvation to towns-people's list of suffering.

However in the midst of all the turmoil and despite the slow deterioration of the castle, over the years York clawed its way back to eventually become the number one city in the North, due to the fact that it held an important strategic position and also was the main market for everything that was bought or sold in the North of England. New buildings were going up right left and centre and the medieval building industry went ballistic.

The Minster was continually being enlarged and heightened with new improvements being added almost daily. Then, like today, it was impossible to see the building without it being covered in scaffolding and tarpaulin. Builders and stone masons worked morning noon and night on the job. To alleviate the boredom and to cover up for the appalling lack of suitable models, they took to carving images of each other. However, as none of the masons actually liked each other, and pretty sure that no one would ever get a stepladder and have a close look at them, they carved a series of satirical grotesques, which is architectural jargon for sculptures that took the piss out of the way each other looked.

The Holy Trinity Church, in Goodramgate was constructed in 1250 on the site of a previous church and throughout this period many other city churches were enlarged and modernised with hot and cold running water in most fonts.

In 1280 the building known as Kings Manor was constructed. This house was originally built as the residence of the Abbot of Saint Mary's, which gives you an indication of how well the monasteries were doing at the time. They also spent money on the building of the Hospitium. Despite its name this building had nothing to do with illness, it was the guest house of the Abbey, (As in hospitality, get it?). This particular period of time must have been a boom time for York builders because, due to pressure of work and a large waiting list they didn't get around to building the second floor of the Hospitium until 1420, over a hundred years later.

This building boom didn't just affect the official and religious buildings. During this period many new residential houses were erected. Lady Row in Goodramgate was built in 1316 and is the earliest example of a building style known as jettied ranges, an architectural name for buildings where the upper floor projects out from the lower floor, and where you bang your head if you're not careful.

Builders weren't the only people doing well. The boom spread throughout the city and the tradesmen, always wary of missing out on a good thing, formed themselves into guilds or, as they would probably be seen these days, restrictive trades practices. Soon it was impossible for anyone to deal in trade or manufacture anything if they weren't a member of a guild. There were trades dedicated to the woollen trade, the cloth trade, the leather trade, and glass makers & blowers. Even the bottom knockers and clinker scrapers had their own guild. Soon just about everything it was possible to trade in was governed by a guild and it comes as no surprise that these guilds soon became very rich and, funded by membership fees, built for themselves fine guildhalls from where they controlled their interests and held parties for their members.

Some of these guildhalls still survive, the Merchant Adventurers' Hall being the finest example. Originally it was founded in 1357 as a religious institution, but soon became the home of the Merchant Adventurers' Company of the City of York, who were granted a licence to operate by Edward III. It seems that the role of this particular guild, who became one of the most powerful in the city, was to attract trade into the city and the surrounding area. A not too dissimilar role to that given to the various local council and governmental sponsored enterprise agencies that try to attract trade to the city today.

Other guilds had their head offices in different parts of the city. The Guildhall of the Merchant Taylors was in Aldwark. The Guild of Butchers was in the Shambles. The Guild of St. Anthony's was in Peasholme Green, and the Guild of Musicians was in a building that stood somewhere near Stonebow, believed to be the site of the present day Fibbers nightclub, the York home of all things musical and some things that are not.

Around 1340 the York Mystery Plays began. These plays were dramatic reconstructions of biblical stories that were staged to narrate these stories to the illiterate population. Mind you it wasn't the peoples fault that they were illiterate. The church and monks held the privilege of reading and writing, and kept it a secret to themselves occasionally allowing members of the ruling classes to have a go. However because printing hadn't been invented and there were no books or newspapers around to read, the people didn't really give a toss.

The Mystery Plays were actually a series of plays featuring biblical stories each performed by a guild that had some tenuous link to their particular trade. For instance, The Creation was performed by the Guild of Midwifery, the New Testament story of changing water into wine was performed by the Threshers Guild, the owners of off-licences and liquor stalls, whilst The Book of Revelation was performed by the Guild of the Four Horsemen, who looked after everything to do with death, pestilence, famine and tax collection in the city.

Some of the smaller guilds didn't have enough members to stage their own plays and so they combined with other small guilds. The Guild of Bakers and Fishermen combined together to perform the story of the loaves and fishes. The Guilds of Cutlers, Bladesmiths, Sheathers, Scalers, Buckle-makers and Horners all combined to perform the Old Testament story about cutting, blading, sheathing, and scaling whilst wearing buckles and blowing horns. Bizarrely the Guild of Butchers got to perform the play about crucifixion.

As so many people wanted to see them and as in those days York had no theatre, all these plays were performed on the backs of decorated carts which were pulled round and round the city in an endless procession by paid labourers, thus giving birth to the concept of a "theatre in the round." The overall effect was something similar to today's modern village fêtes and pageants, only these days the decorated carts are called floats and tend to be pulled by enormous four wheel drive tractors and pantechnicans borrowed for the occasion from the local haulier. Another difference is that these days the religious plays have been replaced by children dressed as Mutant Nija Turtles and Tellytubbies alongside the male members of the local Round Table dressed as female extras from Hello Dolly! Also the mystery plays didn't have a float that carried the spoilt, gloating, thirteen year old daughter of the local council member, laughingly voted this year's carnival queen.

The Mystery Plays were performed on The Feast Day of Corpus Christi, the Thursday that followed Trinity Sunday, straight after St. Ethel's Bagday Monday. This day off was very popular and many people came into the city to eat, drink and be merry, and occasionally stick their heads out of the pub window as another cart load of screaming guild members, spouting their bits of plays were pulled passed.

However if you actually wanted to watch the plays, sustenance and a comfy seat were essential. The first cart played the first venue, outside the Holy Trinity Priory, Micklegate, at five o'clock in the morning and finished at Pavement around noon, just as the last play, The Judgement, was beginning back at the Holy Trinity. They usually got to Pavement around eight in the evening. That meant the populace of York was treated to a non-stop spectacle that lasted for over fifteen hours! For the sake of all our bottoms it is only to be hoped that the nice hero of British cinema Kenneth Brannagh never decides to make them into a film.

Eventually the carts took to stopping at certain points along the way and the local shopkeepers, householders and anyone else who had something to sell, began to offer money to the guilds to stop in front of their establishment. It is recorded that in 1454 the city collected £6 3s 4d in revenue for these pitches.

The funding for these extravaganzas was supplied by the guild members who were forced to pay membership fees that included an additional sum called "pageant silver". Recently it has been discovered that this fee was still being levied on the membership in 1771 - two hundred years after the mystery plays were last performed, a testament to the strength, power and book-keepers of these guilds.

In 1397 the plays were watched by none other than King Richard III who, on one of his state visits to the city, watched them from the Priory in Micklegate inside a specially built pavilion with padded seating. It is worth pondering, (or not, depending on your mood), whether during the fifteen long hours of entertainment, the King ever wondered if anyone would write a play about him.

The Mystery Plays were brought to an end during the Reformation when Protestant clergy decided that the plays contained "suspicious doctrine", in other words they contradicted their own view point. However the Church didn't actually ban the plays, instead in 1572 all the copies were collected by Archbishop Edwin Sandys claiming that he simply wanted to correct them. Strangely enough he never gave them back.

They were eventually revived in 1951 when they were performed on a specially constructed stage built against the spectacular backdrop of St. Mary's Abbey, and have been performed every three years ever since. However due to inclement weather and the rate capping policies of the previous Tory government, the York Council of the stringent cost cutting 1990's, staged them inside the Barbican Theatre. It has been mooted that if there are any further cut backs they will be performed in the official council car park by a solitary mime artist.

Medieval York had many strange inhabitants. In 1348 an apothecary's shoppe opened in St. Helen's Square owned by one Annabel Paxo of The Black Stuff. Originally the church regarded this woman as a witch, especially the then Archbishop of York, Robert

Thoresby. However after she had helped to cure both him and his household from the dreaded "Droppsie Plop", a virulent strain of dysentery common during the 12th century, she was allowed to open a shoppe and ply her trade within the city walls. The site she chose was the new development on the corner of Jubbergate.

She sold a large selection of herbs, self-made potions and rare spices, used in early medicine, many of which were introduced into this country after the First Crusades. Where she developed this knowledge from remains a mystery although it is believed that prior to arriving in York she had some links with The Knights Hospitallers. What those links were is not known although rumour mongers spread the word through York that -

> *"....she would come all over flustered and*
> *wobblie at the sightie of a soldier's*
> *helmet".*

Her most famous concoction was something called "Ye Olde Sage and Onion Potion" which was used for curing piles. It seems that this treatment involved placing large handfuls of the hot steaming mixture on the patients affected parts. It is recorded that once a York resident had been treated by this method they would never complain of piles again - no matter how bad they would get!

The cure eventually died out but her family kept the secret recipe throughout the centuries and re-invented it earlier this century. It never really caught on until, as a joke during a wild game of charades one Christmas lunchtime, a member of the family tried to stuff the mixture up a turkey's bottom. They went on to make a bloody fortune, especially when they tried killing the turkey first.

As well as being treated by apothecaries the sick and injured of medieval England were also treated by men known as "barber surgeons". In 1346, whilst Edward was away on the continent attacking the French, King David of Scotland saw his opportunity and attacked England. Queen Philippa immediately travelled to York to supervise the nation's defence. With her approval an army was raised by the

Archbishop and two northern Lords, Neville and Percy. They marched out and met the Scots in battle near to the city of Durham. After a hard fight the Scots King was captured and his army dispersed. However he was injured by an arrow that became embedded in his cheek bone. On hearing this news Queen Philippa sent two barber surgeons William de Bolton and Hugo de Kilvington from York to treat the wounded prisoner. Using a special remedy they extracted the arrow and managed to heal the wound and were paid the princely sum of £6.00 for their services. The remedy that the barber surgeons used still survives to this day.

To take corns from the feet, and to extract broken needles and arrows from the flesh.

Takie one ounce of wax, quarter ounce of resin and one ounce each of Arstolochia Rotunda and Aristolochia Llonga. Melt the wax and the resin and then add the powder, finely beaten up and sifted, and stir well until the whole thing is cold. Lay it on as a plaster to any injured part, morning and evening. It has been well tried and is a good healer.

This recipe has been adapted through the ages and today is better known by the proprietary brand name of Germoline.

Heady with success the barber surgeons formed themselves into a guild and performed treatments that ranged from hair-cutting to surgery. However their main treatment for just about every disease and illness was phlebotomy, better known as bleeding. To help the blood letting patients were instructed to grip a large pole which made the veins on their arms stand out, making it easier to find them and cut them open. These poles eventually became stained red with blood and were hung outside the premises of barber surgeons as a sort of shop sign. One day a strong wind blew through the city and snapped a number of these poles. Not wanting to replace them the barber surgeons tied bandages around the broken poles to hold them together, thus giving birth to the more familiar red and white striped poles that used to hang outside of barber shops. This practice has now virtually died out with the advent of unisex hair boutiques.

From 1323-1358 the city was occupied by the Wangles, the notorious family of Flemish whelk fettlers who escaped the Wars of the Wasps (1321-1322) in lower Belgium, and came to the City to live and ply their unsavoury trade from a back street near the market place. For many years the painful sounds of screaming whelks being boiled to death echoed across Jubbergate, until one night the neighbours, being both drunk and vegetarian, gathered up a mob of like minded folk and drove the family out of the city. Angered at being driven out of their comfy dwelling and having to take to the road once again, the leader of the family laid his curse upon the City of York. Ten years to the very day a plague of boils broke out. Ever since then it has been impossible to find a decently boiled whelk inside the walls of York.

Another strange inhabitant of the medieval city was a person believed to have been Robin Hood's illegitimate brother, a man named Robbin' Bastard. Instead of robbing from the rich to give to the poor this man would rob from the poor and leave the small amount of coin he gained on the doorsteps of York's rich and famous. Unfortunately this coin was so small that the rich and famous thought they had dropped some small change and never realised that it was the work of a twisted benefactor.

Robbin' Bastard died in obscurity, although in later years as his fame grew he became the patron saint of tax collectors, VAT inspectors, council tax officials, car clampers, and the many other robbing bastards who to this day continue the tradition of taking from the poor and giving to the rich.

Whilst the Black Death was killing off a third of the population, Edward was away in France fighting a series of battles and wars that became known as The Hundred Years War. He became King of France in 1340, but there was very little money to finance the rest of his fighting and towards the end of 1340 he returned to England to demand some more money from the government. In a fit of petulance he sacked his Chancellor, Robert Stratford and many other government officials.

Eventually as soon as he got his hands on more money he went straight back to France.

That same year Northern England came under attack from King David of the Scots who had waited for his moment until Edward was busy fighting the Battle of Crecy. Having won his battle Edward returned to England to attack and defeat the Scots. In his absence he left his son in France, who was known as the Black Prince due to his active dislike of washing. By 1358 Edward had beaten the Scots into submission and he went back to France. Father and son then spent the next twenty odd years happily criss-crossing the channel fighting either the French or the Scots.

However over the years the French fought back and by 1376 Edward had lost most of his conquests. He had also lost the respect of the English population. The people of England were getting pretty fed up of stumping up for the King's exploits and his losses. Parliament openly criticised the King's spending in 1371, 1372, 1373. In 1376 they finally got fed up of letting him off with a warning, showed him the red card, and actually impeached a number of royal officials.

Edward's reaction to his sending off was to promptly lie down and die. The Black Prince would have been next in line to the throne, only he had died some months before his father, and so the throne passed onto his son, Edward's grandson, Richard II.

Richard was only ten years of age when he got the job and his court was overshadowed by his three royal uncles, Edmund of Langley, The Duke of York; Thomas of Woodstock, the Duke of Gloucester; and John of Gaunt, the Duke of Lancaster who, instead of helping the poor kid to run the country, promptly began a power struggle that raged for the next hundred years.

In 1380 the continuing lack of royal funds forced Richard to instigate a new tax which he chose to call the Poll Tax. For the hard pressed peasants of England this new tax was about as welcome as a fart in a sleeping bag. In Essex they refused to pay up and took a man called Wat Tyler as their leader. He led them on a rampage through

Rochester and Canterbury before marching on London where they burnt the Archbishop's Palace at Lambeth and devastated Southwark. The fourteen year old King bravely rode out to meet the mob at Mile End and attempted to negotiate with them. He promised a fifty hour week with every other weekend off, the abolition of villeinage, money back on all empty beer bottles, and a pension plan linked to profit share. Some went off home, pleased with getting a result, but the more extreme hard liners followed Wat Tyler to the Tower of London, dragged the Archbishop of Canterbury from his prayers and beheaded him on Tower Hill. As if that wasn't enough a couple of days later they grabbed a royal official from Westminster Abbey and executed him in the City.

This was taking industrial disputes too far and the young King agreed to meet with the rebels once more. He was just about to agree to further terms when the Lord Mayor of London, fed up with all the indecisive chat, took matters into his own hands and rammed his sword through Wat Tyler's chest. That was that, and the rebellion in London was over. As with today, fashion trends that originate in London take some time to filter to the rest of the country and, after the men of Kent had packed up and gone home, troubles broke out in St. Albans, Bury St. Edmonds and Norwich.

Another similarity with today is that the promises made by the management weren't worth the parchment they were written on and all the promises made at Mile End were never honoured, which really didn't come as a great surprise to anyone. Mind you, the peasants did have one small success. The government conveniently forgot all about the Poll Tax and it disappeared for another six hundred years or so when it was re-introduced by Margaret Thatcher's Conservative government around 1990. Oh, Wat Tyler where were you when your country needed you then?

For the next ten years Richard concentrated on building up a reputation for good government and getting on the right side of the English people. He came to a peaceful agreement with France, and rationalised the government of Ireland. He also encouraged the arts and became friends with William Caxton. A little known fact about Richard is that he was the first English monarch to carry a handkerchief. Not a lot of people know that!

The death of his wife Queen Anne in 1394 was the beginning of his end. He increasingly became more and more paranoid. You know the sort of thing. It starts off by having to check that you've locked the front door at least three times before you go out. Then you're convinced that you've left the oven on, usually when you're a hundred miles from home. Eventually it builds up so much that you end up thinking that everyone is out to get you. Mind you, in the case of medieval royalty, they usually were! As his paranoia increased Richard raised his own army and in 1397 attacked the Lords Appellants. To show that he didn't believe in nepotism he impeached his Uncle Gloucester and exiled him to Calais where he was conveniently murdered. Then just to prove the point he executed Lord Arundel and arranged for the three remaining Lords Appellants to be exiled.

He returned to Ireland and, as soon as his back was turned, one of the exiled Lords, Henry Bolingbroke, gathered up an army and sailed back from France. He landed in the North of England, at the mouth of the Humber, and persuaded the people of the North to join up with him. By the time Richard returned from his Irish golfing holiday the House of Lancaster had usurped the throne and Bolingbroke had declared himself Henry IV. Richard was imprisoned in the Tower before being carted off to Pontefract Castle where he died "under mysterious circumstances".

Mind you, getting hold of the crown proved to be a lot easier than actually holding onto it, as Henry IV was about to find out. In his first nine years of rule Henry faced rebellions from all directions. Owen Glendower wound up the Welsh. Armies gathered along the Scottish border. Heretics questioned the authority of the church, and Henry even managed to fall out with his own son. Finally when he fell into the now familiar trap of thinking that things couldn't get any worse, they did. A crowd of young ambitious Earls who were too young to fight in the last shindig began to pressurise him into re-starting a war with France. It was enough to make him turn grey, which he did just before dying in 1413 aged only 47.

Henry IV, surprisingly enough, was followed by his son Henry V who was famous for beating France at Agincourt in 1415 and who was recognised as regent of France. He married Catherine of Valois, daughter of the French King and was next in line for the French monarchy which would have united England and France under one King. Unfortunately, just after the birth of his own son Henry V contracted dysentery and died. Showing a remarkable ineptitude for imagination when it came to naming children, Henry's son had also called Henry and so, on the death of his father, became Henry VI.

Having an infant on the English throne didn't do much for the stability of the country. Once again the powerful Lords of England plotted, schemed and curried favour. Henry became little more than a pawn in the heaviest game of power politics you could imagine. However he did manage to stay on the throne for many years until, in 1453, the entire thing became too much for him and he became deranged. His wife Queen Margaret tried to take the reigns of power herself, but Parliament showed their sexist face and gave preference to Richard Duke of York, thus starting the outbreak of a series of conflicts and battles which lasted from 1455 to 1485 and that are now known as "The Wars of the Roses".

Richard of York was killed at the Battle of Wakefield in 1460, and showing a peculiar attack of bad taste, Queen Margaret had a paper crown placed on his severed head and stuck it on a sharp pole above York's Micklegate Bar. Thus giving Shakespeare one of his better known jokes -

"So York may look upon York!"

Today, with our more refined sense of humour and the advent of alternative stand-up comedians such as Ben Elton, Jo Brand and Eddie Izzard, that line may not seem very funny, but when it was first performed in Elizabethan times it had them rolling in the aisles. In fact it is said that Shakespeare himself nearly wet himself just writing it!

A couple of months after the Battle of Wakefield Richard's eldest son Edward led an army into London and was crowned Edward IV.

Later that year Margaret and Henry, leading a huge army, fought Edward at the Battle of Towton, just down the A1 from York where the road has being turned into a multi-lane highway.

This battle is claimed to be the largest and most bloody battle ever fought on English soil. It was certainly the only one fought on a Palm Sunday in the middle of a snowstorm. The Yorkist faction had the home advantage and chose to wear their normal strip of white. The Lancastrians, playing away, had to wear their away strip which was red. Obviously fighting the battle in the middle of a snowstorm the Yorkists held a distinct advantage - they couldn't be seen! At one point the tables seemed to be turned. So much blood was shed that the snow turned red and then it was the Lancastrians that couldn't be seen. Unfortunately, as most of the blood was Lancastrian it didn't make much difference and they were routed. Margaret and Henry fled to Scotland whilst the victorious Edward travelled to London and just to make sure, on mid-summer's day got himself crowned Edward IV once again (or should it have been Edward V as this was his second time around?).

One of Edward's leading supporters and advisors was his cousin the Earl of Warwick known as "The Kingmaker". Warwick clearly had plans for the young King but, as soon as he was crowned, Edward dispensed with Warwick's advice and secretly married Lady Elizabeth Woodville, a widow of a Lancastrian Baron. Warwick sulked, took his bat and ball home, and in 1469 gathered himself an army. Edward fled to Holland and Henry VI was restored to the throne. (This part of his reign should have been called Henry VI Part Two, however for reasons best known to himself Shakespeare decided to give that title to Henry IV; perhaps he got his Roman numerals mixed up.)

Despite his taking advantage of his help, Henry and Margaret didn't trust Warwick one bit, and before they knew what was happening Edward had managed to get a small army together and invaded England. He captured Henry and imprisoned him in the Tower of London then went on to defeat and kill Warwick at the Battle of Barnet in 1471, and London offered him the crown once again. Three weeks later Margaret was defeated at the battle of Tewkesbury. By a strange quirk of fate Henry was murdered in the Tower of London the night after the battle, just after Edward returned to London - odd that isn't it?.

To say that Edward was ruthless is stating the obvious: he had to be. Being King was a tough job, but someone had to do it. There was no one you could trust and everyone was out to get you. Mind you, one person he did trust was his younger brother Richard, Duke of Gloucester whom he appointed as protector of the kingdom and of its heir, Edward's twelve year old son cunningly named (yes you've guessed it!) Edward.

Richard was also promoted to the position of Constable and Admiral of England, with a special authority to look after the North of England. He promptly set up for business in York and got himself a nice weekend house overlooking the sea at Scarborough. However Edward's other brother, The Duke of Clarence, was proving to be a bit of a problem. Edward refused him permission to marry a woman called Mary of Burgundy, probably because her father had refused to help Edward invade France. The Duke had a fit of the sulks and ran off to East Anglia where he got involved in an uprising that Edward quickly stamped out. The Duke was imprisoned in the Tower, but being the brother of the King must have given him certain privileges because during his incarceration the Duke was given a barrel of wine to drink. Unfortunately someone must have forgotten to give the unfortunate Duke a glass or even a mug to drink from and he was forced to drink out of the barrel. He must have made the same mistake as a lot of people do when they drink wine - he drank too much too fast. Then, as he was trying to get the last few drinks out of the bottom of the barrel, he fell in, got stuck and drowned. At least that was the story put about at the time! This event acted as a dire warning to all Barons not to upset Edward or to try to drink wine from the bottom of a barrel.

This warning must have worked because in England things quietened down for a while, although in Scotland things got very hairy. As Edward had made his brother Richard responsible for the North it was deemed his problem and, whilst The Duke of Gloucester fought tooth and nail all over The Borders, Edward got on with running the rest of the Kingdom and enjoying himself with his many mistresses.

Richard finally captured Edinburgh and the Scots surrendered to him in August 1482. For his troubles he was promoted to Governer of Carlisle and Cumberland, but he barely had time to put his feet up as Edward died in 1483 and the old familiar power struggle broke out once again.

The family of the younger Edward tried to rush through a quick coronation, and didn't invite Richard who retaliated by capturing the young prince and his even younger brother and hiding them in the Tower of London. Then when everyone was busy looking for them, Richard managed to muddy the waters over the question of succession by questioning the validity of Edward's marriage.

The trick worked. Some loophole was found in the law that clearly stated Edward wasn't married at all, although there were more than a few people who swore blind that they could remember being there. A knock on the door in the middle of the night soon made them realise that it must have been someone else's wedding they had been to. Eventually the marriage was deemed to be invalid, the children were declared illegitimate, and Richard was declared King Richard III.

Whatever happened to the two princes in the Tower still remains a mystery to this day. Over the years many theories have been put forward. One states that they ran off and joined a travelling circus, another claims that they were roasted in oil and then eaten by their vicious Uncle. Yet another claims that they were put to sleep by a wicked witch, woken by a kiss from a record executive in the nineteen nineties and changed their names to Liam and Noel Gallaher. No one knows for certain what happened other than that they were never seen again.

CHAPTER EIGHT

TUDOR YORK

The Middle Ages came to an end when Henry Tudor, Duke of Richmond, killed Richard III at the Battle of Bosworth, and despite having no legal claim to the kingdom, grabbed the throne for himself, thus becoming Henry VII. So powerfully did he grab it and hold onto it that his family ruled England for the next 118 years.

Richard III was one of the most maligned Kings ever unfortunate enough to sit on the English throne. In today's society we would say that he suffered from a "bad press". Even Shakespeare slagged him off, portraying him as a physically deformed monster capable of committing any horrendous crime. Mind you it has to be remembered that most of the writers who portrayed him were working under the rule of the Tudor dynasty and, as all freelance writers know, you don't bite the hand that feeds you, especially if it belongs to royalty. Their motivation was "to hell with accuracy as long as the invoice gets paid", and no Tudor monarch would pay for a story that praised the merits of the bloke their family had just killed and chucked off the throne.

Richard III had reigned for two years when Henry Tudor, the sole Lancastrian claimant to the throne, sailed with an army gathered in France and landed at Milford Haven. The two met in battle at Bosworth field in 1485, and despite never having been in a battle before, Henry won the day and Richard III became the first English king to be killed in battle since King Harold. That makes you think - all that fighting and battling and not one fatality in 419 years, whilst thousands of barons, lords, earls, dukes, knights and sundry others formed a line of dead bodies that would stretch from London to Scotland five times over.

Henry's victory was unexpected, indeed the bookies of the time had him as a 33/1 outsider for the throne mainly due to the fact that the young King had hardly ever been to England. In his twenty eight years he spent half his time in Wales and the rest in Brittany but, despite this unfamiliarity with the country, he managed to rule it quiet successfully for the next twenty four years.

In 1486 he married Elizabeth of York, the eldest child of Edward IV's, hoping the act would placate the House of York, and at least allow him to turn his back on them now and then. It didn't! Despite having a family member as Queen the Yorkist faction were still sculking and plotting in the shadows. One of the Yorkist plots was to get a young man named Perkin Warbeck to try and pass himself off as the younger of the two Princes who disappeared in the Tower, but everyone saw through his disguise when they realised that Warbeck looked nothing like the missing Prince, was left handed and spoke with a different accent.

Warbeck visited Scotland and Ireland, trying to drum up support in the rural areas that had never seen the young prince. He eventually landed in Cornwall, where communications were so sparse that they didn't even know that Henry was king. Warbeck's silver tongue won the day and he was proclaimed King Richard IV at Bodmin, then he made a tactical mistake. He stepped out of Cornwall and a month later he was captured, brought to Henry as a prisoner and was executed in 1499.

Despite the abrupt manner in which he came to the throne Henry VII was not the sort of king who jumped onto his horse waving his sword about at the first sign of trouble. Nor did he go out of his way looking for it. Instead he strengthened his position, and the country, by creating a good, solid and effective administration. Something never really tried by an English King before.

He gave the existing administrative system a thorough overhauling that had the same effect as mending a microprocessor with a three inch wrench. By the time he had finished he'd swept away half of the old barons from the King's Council and banned anyone from having their own private army, except himself. He spread his power about by reforming and extending the local duties of Justices of The Peace, and more or less, for better or worse, created the concept of local government.

Unlike most of his predecessors Henry VII wasn't interested in party, party, party, he was interested in trade and helped to secure good deals for English merchants abroad. He was also determined to make the crown solvent again. The first thing he arranged was to audit his own books. That came as a shock to a lot of people, especially those who had access to the Royal coffers. For the first time in English history a King saw precisely what amounts of money were being spent on his behalf. Suddenly throughout all the administration offices of Royal castles orders for office stationery were stopped, all luncheon vouchers were cancelled, and keys suddenly appeared on all petty cash tins.

Henry became so cost conscious that he realised he could make savings on a round of job rationalisations. As a result he appointed his friend Morton as both Archbishop of Canterbury and Chancellor of England, a sort of job share with a difference, one man sharing two jobs.

Realising that he couldn't rely just on cost savings to make ends meet Henry got Morton to increase tax revenues by coming up with an ingenious theory called "Morton's Fork". This theory worked as follows: If someone appeared to enjoy a lavish lifestyle it was screamingly obvious that they weren't paying enough tax, so they had to pay some more. If someone else lived a prudent and thrifty lifestyle it was obvious that they were saving their money, and if they were saving money they could afford to pay more tax.

It was the perfect "Heads I win, tails you lose!" situation. It was so successful that when Henry came to the throne the crown was in debt, when he died twenty four years later the books showed a credit balance of a million and a half pounds.

Henry wasn't a tight arse though. Behind his public mask of austerity he enjoyed many luxuries and expensive pleasures. He financed the voyage of the explorer John Cabot who claimed to discover Newfoundland thinking he had discovered the coast of Asia. When he arrived back in London Henry gave him ten pounds, a pension of twenty pounds a year and financed his next voyage, in exchange for one fifth of the resulting profits.

Henry also spent money building Richmond Palace, a chapel in Westminster Abbey and, in an act of pure frivolity, bought a leopard for the menagerie in the Tower of London. Even his kids did well. Not for them some arranged marriage to a decrepit, hairy arsed northern baron in the hope that bedding the King's daughter would ensure peace for a few weeks. Oh no! Henry's two daughters married The King of France and the King of Scotland. His eldest son Arthur married Catherine of Aragon, the joint ruler of Spain.

It must also be noted that Henry also had the good sense to name his heir Arthur. This was probably because he knew he was beginning a Tudor dynasty and that he wanted to use different names so that people wouldn't get them all mixed up, or have to learn Roman numerals. It was also so that everyone knew that Henry VI started it off and his memory wouldn't be over shadowed by anyone else with the same name. Then Henry went and blew it. Thinking he was safe he named his second son Henry. As we all know, fate has a nasty habit of sticking its two fingers up to the best laid plans of mice and men. Although what plans mice have to make I've yet to work out. Anyway, five months after his marriage young Arthur died of consumption and so the next in line to the throne of England was yet another bloody Henry, probably the most bloody of all, Henry VIII!

As Henry VII had invested heavily in a time-share holiday villa in Southern Spain he still wanted to keep on good terms with the Spanish throne and so he married his second son to the widow of his first. Suddenly instead of being young Henry's sister in law Catherine was now his wife, and we all know what happened next.

Henry VII died in 1509 and, in the now familiar and traditional manner, Henry VIII took over the Kingdom. At the start of his rule it was business as usual. In 1513 he strengthened his alliance and fought a brief war in France. But soon he found more pleasurable pursuits and handed the running of the country over to Thomas Wolsey who took the concept of job share a step further by becoming Archbishop of York, a Cardinal and Lord Chancellor. It was he who stage managed the media event known as "The Field of the Cloth of Gold" which was a four week long party held near Calais where Henry VIII and Francis I the King of

France indulged themselves by showing off to each other, taking photo opportunities, watching jousts, eating banquets, hunting, drinking and chasing women.

This lifestyle suited Henry who liked to project an image of an able huntsman, an expert at martial arts, and a scholar and musician. He even turned his hand to writing and was the first English ruler to have a book published when he wrote "In Defence of the Seven Sacraments". Pope Leo X was so impressed with this slim volume that he gave Henry the title "Defender of the Faith" and made the book "editor's choice of the month" in the Vatican Book Club.

But no matter what literary or musical heights the King achieved, in true tabloid tradition, he will for ever be remembered as that bearded fat bloke who had six wives, and who was played by Keith Michelle in the popular television series "The Six Wives of Henry VIII". So let's take a deep breath and quickly go through it all.

Catherine of Aragon gave birth to a son, but he only lived for six weeks. There followed a series of miscarriages and still births, the birth of a daughter, but no son. Henry convinced himself that this was God's judgement for marrying his own sister in law and so he asked Wolsey to sort out an annulment with the Pope. Whilst these delicate negotiations were going on Henry met and fell in love with Anne Boleyn, the twenty year old daughter of the Lord Mayor of London.

The Pope refused the divorce, not for religious reasons but mainly because he was under the control of Emperor Charles V, who just happened to be Catherine's nephew. Wolsey's failure to sort the problem out got him the sack and he was replaced by Thomas Cromwell who came up with the idea of formally separating the English Church from papal control, thus allowing the primate of England, Archbishop Thomas Cranmer to declare the marriage null and void.

Under Cromwell's management a Reformation Parliament of 1529-36 was set up that was sympathetic to the King's desires. This Parliament declared that Henry was now the Supreme Head of the Church in England. In 1536 and 1539 the Parliament arranged for the dissolution of all the monasteries in England and the lands and properties that they owned to be divided among themselves and other interested parties.

Whilst all that was going on Anne Boleyn gave birth to a daughter, but failed to deliver a male heir. Henry then convinced himself that the woman had other lovers and on May 1536 she was tried and executed on trumped up charges of treason.

Eleven days later Henry (he didn't believe in hanging around this one!) married the daughter of a Wiltshire knight, the famous actress Jane Seymour. She did give birth to a son (later to become Edward VI), but unfortunately Jane did not survive the birth and died in 1537.

It can be said in Henry's favour that he allowed himself a couple of years as a widower before falling in love with a portrait of a woman called Anne of Cleeves. However when she arrived at the English Court Henry realised what artistic licence was all about. The painting had been more than flattering and, in real life, the woman was plain looking. Worse than that, she couldn't speak English and had appalling manners. She farted in bed, ate with her elbows on the table, and scratched her crutch in public. Having met her once Henry realised his mistake and never went anywhere near her again and the marriage was quickly dissolved.

Shortly after Anne had been sent away Henry bumped into Catherine Howard, a cousin of Anne Boleyn, and promptly fell in love again. As a young girl Catherine was York's most eligible beauty and inheritor of nearby Castle Howard. She frequently used to shop at York market and always popped into local cafés for a cuppa tea and a sticky bun. The buns weren't meant to be sticky, it was just that there had been an unfortunate accident in the kitchens.

When Catherine married Henry VIII on 28th July 1540, the citizens of York joined in the festivities with a vengeance. A huge street party was held in Jubbergate where musicians and troubadours played for three straight days and four bent knights. A poster from this period cites that -

"A reet jollie and merrie do will occur
on the celebration of our Cathy's marriage
to yon King Henry. Musical delights
will be provided by ye famous band
of York musicians The Orphans of Aldo."

However, Catherine proved to be even more indiscreet than her cousin and the poor girl fell victim to Henry's extreme views about separation and divorce. She was executed in Feb. 1542 by her head being separated from her body and York mourned the loss of a daughter and a damn good shopper. This unfortunate occurrence was celebrated by the BBC a few years ago when they made their famous television period drama "Bride's Head Revisited" filmed ironically at Castle Howard.

The following year Henry once again fell in love and married a lady named Catherine Parr, who had already buried two husbands herself and was an expert in survival techniques, a handy knack to have in the King's court. Catherine managed to survive the last four years of Henry's life when the King, once a handsome young man, had turned into a bitter and twisted, argumentative and obese tyrant.

During the reign of Henry VIII many scientific discoveries were made. One of these was the discovery that if you poured sulphuric acid onto limestone the stone would melt. After falling out with the church, who told him he couldn't keep on divorcing and remarrying (they didn't seem to mind the chopping off of heads as that was a matter of civil law and nothing to do with them), Henry and his men began to travel around England pouring this acid onto religious buildings, thus we have the event in history known as the Dissolution of the Monasteries.

At the beginning of Henry VIII's reign, as well as the Minster, York boasted two large monastic buildings, St. Mary's Abbey and the Priory of Holy Trinity, Micklegate. It also had forty parish churches, six hospitals and almshouses, two friaries, two nunneries, and half a dozen chapels. It had guild halls, stone built mansions, and lots of other houses. In short it was a thriving and prosperous city.

After the dissolution of the monasteries the place came to resemble a ghost town. St. Mary's Abbey, St. Leonard's and the Holy Trinity Priory had closed, along with the various nunneries, chapels, and sixteen parish churches. Many traders and merchants who held contracts with the religious houses went bankrupt. To make matters worse the workforce was suddenly doubled by the numbers of ex-monks who were all seeking work. Suddenly the waiting area of the Benefits Office looked like a penguin colony, what with all the out of work monks and nuns queuing up to sign on. It is safe to say that Henry's Dissolution of the Monasteries affected York almost as badly as AB&B's "Dissolution of the Railway Works" did in 1996/7.

To make matters worse the River Ouse was beginning to silt up, just at the same time as ships were getting bigger. In consequence the town began to lose its importance as a major port. More and more ships began to off-load further down river at Hull, claiming that it saved a couple of days' sailing, saved on the sailors' wages and anyway Hull had a better nightlife. If cargoes had to be sent on to York from Hull they were re-loaded into smaller boats called lighters (because they carried a lighter weight) and sent up river along with an invoice for loading and unloading. When the York traders and merchants saw this invoice they thought that the dockers of Hull were taking the piss. They had a point, after all they hadn't asked for the goods to be unloaded. But, no matter how much they objected, the dockers of Hull had them by the short and curlies. If they didn't pay up the goods would be left to rot on the Hull quayside. Eventually they paid up but the bad feeling between the two towns still remains to this day.

To use current "politician speak", if the Dissolution of the Monasteries and the loss of port revenue was a double whammy for York, the decline of the woollen industry hit York like a rabbit punch from that big wrestler person called Giant Haystacks. Throughout the 13th and 14th centuries York was one of the largest cloth producing centres in England. Over a quarter of its residents earned a living from its manufacture. By 1517 weaving wasn't even listed in the top thirteen most popular jobs of York. In 1561 there were only ten weavers left, a few years later there were none. So what happened? Water power, that's what happened.

Some bright spark living in Leeds realised that they could use water power to turn the wheels and cogs which powered fulling machines. Soon the cloth trade moved to places like Halifax, Wakefield and of course, Leeds. Ah ha! I hear you say, why didn't the cloth makers of York all get together and build their own water powered fulling machines? Better still, why didn't they just pop over to Leeds and steal one?

Remember what I said about the Ouse silting up? Well a silted up river doesn't flow very fast, and water driven fulling machines need fast running water to drive them, not the sticky porridge like substance that the Ouse had become.

Another advantage West Yorkshire had over York was that the woollen industry wasn't controlled by restrictive trades practices. There were no guilds to set a fair day's wages for a fair day's pay, no social contract, no knocking off at five o'clock, and no organised workforce who could threaten to strike at any slight upset. All these factors made West Yorkshire the perfect place for capitalist minded merchants and manufacturers to set up the woollen industry and bide their time waiting for the Industrial Revolution when they could really cash in on cheap, unskilled, non-unionised labour.

As if things weren't bad enough, just as the city was coming to its senses from Giant Haystacks' rabbit punch another economic blow hit York right between its blinking eyes. The city began to run out of fuel. As long as the city had been populated whenever anyone needed any fuel they popped over the walls and chopped down the nearest tree. As York was surrounded by the huge forest of Galtres this wasn't perceived as much of a problem. However as the city developed, more and more wood was needed and the forest began to shrink further away from the city. By the time Henry VIII came along the only way you could see any forest was by standing on top of the Minster, and anyone who wanted to cut wood got a travel allowance.

Then just to rub the people of York's noses even further in the mire it was discovered that coal was the new fuel of the age, and guess where the coal was? You've got it! It was underneath the West Riding cities of Leeds, Wakefield and Pontefract! It was enough to make a York person spit. It was enough to make grown men bang their heads on the wall until it stopped hurting. Despite half of York's unemployed desperately digging shafts all over the city there was no trace of any coal: West Yorkshire had the lot.

The subsequent rise in unemployment created many problems in York. Not only was the city full of its own poor, but other poor people from the surrounding countryside also flocked into the city in a vain attempt to find work or at least to beg in better surroundings. In 1515 the York Corporation, in a far sighted approach for this period, attempted to introduce a type of Poor Law Act. It is worth commenting that it took another 50 years before such a law was passed by Elizabeth I for the rest of the country.

The York Corporation issued badges that were worn by the "deserving poor". These were a classification of people who through disease, illness or injury were not deemed capable of working. They wore their badge proudly "upon the shoulder of their outermost garment". This badge gave them official permission to beg openly in the city's streets. Other poor people, who the authorities deemed capable of working, were called "sturdy beggars". In a truly enlightened approach to the problem, any poor person who attempted to beg without a licence was flogged and thrown out of the city, usually accompanied by jeers and heckles from the other beggars who were all wearing their official badges.

As more and more beggars flooded into York the Corporation began to lose count of them all and so, in order to keep track of them, they established a new council run position. A number of them were given the title of "Master Beggars" and were appointed in each ward of the city. Their duty was to count the licensed beggars, snitch on any unlicensed ones and report any newcomers to the authorities. They were issued with a special cloak which carried the City's Coat Of Arms and a large springy birch rod with which they asserted their authority, usually across some unfortunates back.

Life for York residents was not good. In fact it was very bad. Industry and jobs were disappearing fast and, just as everyone was walking around saying things couldn't get any worse, as usual they did! In 1538 the city suffered its first outbreak of plague. The narrow, vermin infested streets were perfect breeding places for the disease to grow, fester and spread throughout the city. The worst attacks were in 1538, 1550-52, 1570, and 1579.

In 1552 the city authorities laid down stringent rules and regulations in an attempt to control the disease. Food was to be delivered to houses affected by the plague and left outside on the doorstep. Red crosses were painted on the front doors of the affected households, and everyone tried to avoid them "like the plague", which is probably where the saying came from in the first place. Medical advice was radical - anyone suspected of suffering from the disease was made to wear a long pointed hat with a little bell on the top and was forced to stay in their houses until they either died or got better. Usually it was the former.

Given this set of economic and medical disasters it is very apparent to see why, throughout the Tudor Period, the residents of York were not exactly wearing their happy hats.

Henry VIII survived one large uprising during his reign and that originated in the north. This uprising was called "The Pilgrimage of Grace", named after Grace, the mother of Robert Aske a lawyer and the leader of the rebellion. He marched into York at the head of a group of pilgrims that numbered somewhere between 20-40,000 people.

Aske, together with around 2,000-3,000 horsemen, was allowed inside the city and was welcomed into the Minster by the clergy. They left the city and marched towards Pontefract, forcing the Abbot of St. Mary's to lead them as he was the only person who had ever been there before and who knew that way. Eventually though the rebellion was crushed. The pilgrims were given "false assurances", historian speak for saying that they were lied to. They disbanded and Robert Aske was arrested and condemed to death by being hung in a cage suspended from Clifford's Tower. He took more than a week to die and his body remained hanging in the cage for more than a year, just to persuade anyone from thinking that a rebellion was a good idea.

This uprising alerted Henry to the unrest in the north and so, just to keep an eye on them, he re-instituted "The King's Council In The North". The leader of this council was one Robert Holgate who was promoted to the position of Kings Lieutenant in the North on the condition that he actually lived there. As the monasteries had been dissolved there were plenty of large, ex-religious properties lying empty, just waiting to be lived in and Robert chose to live in the house once owned by the Abbot of St. Mary's which was promptly renamed King's Manor.

Despite the economic gloom hanging over the city this move once again made York top northern city, and as a result brought many visitors to the city. New hotels and bed and breakfast establishments were opened. Overnight the small inns and boarding houses in the city became full to overflowing and many new premises were established. Soon the streets of the city were full of people speaking strange regional accents and the smell of all day breakfasts being fried. Another benefit to the city was that with all these visitors arriving someone had to sell them sticks of rock, small pot figures, funny hats, badges and other tourist knick knacks for which York is so justly famous. In consequence, all the unemployed of the City were gathered up and sent on government training courses to be trained in the new, genteel art of tourism.

Henry VIII died in the January of 1547 and was succeeded by his nine year old son Edward, called for convenience's sake Edward VI. For the first part of this young lad's reign the country was governed by his mother's brother, The Protector, Edward Seymour, Duke of Somerset. The Duke showed some degree of religious tolerance, and even had that rare thing in a person of his elevation, a social conscience, which he aimed like a dart against the greed of the English landowners. However history tells us that Somerset soon succumbed to temptation and became greedy himself. As Edward also disliked him intensely, it came as no surprise that he was deposed in 1549 and eventually executed.

He was replaced by the Duke of Northumberland who had none of Somerset's redeeming qualities. He was ambitious and used his position of power to his best advantage, and all things considered, was ideally qualified to be a 20th century politician.

Northumberland persuaded Edward to sign documents that altered the succession of the throne so as to exclude his Roman Catholic half sister Mary. Instead the successor was to be Henry VIII's great niece Lady Jane Grey, fifth in line to the throne and to whom Northumberland had married his own son, entirely by coincidence of course!

Ten months after signing the document Edward died of tuberculosis, aged only fifteen, and on his death Lady Jane was proclaimed Queen. However, Northumberland's game had been rumbled and the entire country stood behind Mary Tudor as she was escorted into London to claim the throne. It is worth noting that when I use the phrase "the entire country stood behind......" I do not mean it in the literal sense, I was using historian speak again. Despite having their support, very few people actually bothered to travel to London to stand up and be counted. Indeed it is very likely that in some more rural parts of the country the people not only didn't know who the King or Queen was, they probably didn't give a tuppeny damn!

Anyway, back to the plot. Mary was determined to restore the power of the Roman Catholic Church. Legislation seeking a reconciliation was passed through Parliament, although the property rights and interests of the newly rich owners of once monastic lands were looked after and well protected. However word had eventually filtered out to the country, and the same people who would have cheered her into London if they'd bothered to show up, now slowly began to change their minds. Especially as they suddenly realised that she was married to the King of Spain and she wanted him to be regarded as King of England.

As always in cases like this the true English grit and stiff upper lips came to the fore. You can almost hear the old barons, sitting around in their Knightsbridge clubs reciting such quaintly English sayings as: "What, ruled by a bloody dago...?" and "Johnny Foreigner sitting on the throne of England! Over my dead body......". Given a similar set of circumstances today you could easily imagine what the front page of The Sun newspaper would say, especially considering the xenophobic headlines they ran during the Euro Cup of 1996!

The rejection of her husband incited Mary into getting her own back on her subjects and she revived laws that allowed heretics to be burnt at the stake. Soon fires were springing up all over England as many people died in the flames of a hideous human bar-b-que fuelled by quasi religious bigotry and political expediency.

Mary Tudor died in 1558 and was succeed by Elizabeth who almost single handedly nurtured the infant English nation-state, and transformed it from a squawling spoilt brat into the sort of adult maturity that we still know and love today - almost!

CHAPTER NINE

ELIZABETHAN YORK.

As the town of York once again began to increase in importance some of its more fortunate citizens became rich, especially those who had managed to get their hands on the lands and property of the dispossessed religious orders. Property quickly changed hands and before the ordinary people could say "mortgage", they discovered that the land hungry members of the aristocracy had got there before them and grabbed the lot.

The story of the fate of the Archbishop's Palace is one that will make any modern conservationist shudder with self righteous indignation. The original building was a sprawling mass of medieval offices and housing, built on the land to the north west of the Minster.

In the mid 1560's Archbishop Young, who was also President of the Council of the North, decided that his spoilt son should live in the style to which he had become accustomed and arranged for him to have an endowment PEP. In order to get his hands on the cash to form this legacy the Archbishop sold the lead from the roof of Archbishop's Palace. Surprisingly enough the result of this action was water pouring down the inside walls of the building. Soon damp made the palace uninhabitable and, in 1570, the succeeding Archbishop, unable to get the lead back, was forced to build himself a new palace.

As this new Archbishop liked messing about in boats he opted to have his new palace built some miles down the river at Bishopthorpe, just so he could commute by boat.

In 1616 the ruins of the old palace were sold to Sir Arthur Ingram who demolished what was left of the original building and constructed himself a fine new mansion, complete with pleasure gardens, an orchard, a bowling green, walks and fish pond. It is claimed that

Charles I stayed there in 1642, but there again, find me any stately home or mansion that Charles I hasn't stayed in. Today in the grounds of the Minster the only surviving pieces of the original palace are a bit of 12th century arcade and the chapel which is now used as the Minster Library.

Other great houses were built in the city. In the Bishophill area of the town the Duke of Buckingham built a great mansion, which was demolished in the eighteenth century.

In 1600 the existing mediaeval Treasurer's House was demolished and a private house built on the site. Despite these ostentatious displays of wealth the majority of York's population still lived in poverty, but they still knew how to enjoy themselves and, during the reign of Elizabeth I, the citizens found a new entertainment - theatre.

On the corner of Jubbergate, a small hostelry called "The Artichoke" opened up a small balcony theatre where the famous York playwright Albert Waveysticke wrote some of his world famous plays. It is very likely that the romantic prose of his tragic love story "Trevor and Julie", his historical play "Henry IV parts Seven to Eight", his play about the invention of the cigar called "Hamlet" and his fantasy "A Midwinter Morning's Nightmare" were all written on those very premises.

Unfortunately the York audiences, more used to the live music and drunken carousels held in the majority of other York pubs, didn't take kindly to literature being stuffed down their throats. Night after night they packed the stalls and galleries of the Artichoke to boo, hiss and heckle their way through another evening's performance of yet another of Albert Waveysticke's plays. No sooner had an actor marched onto the stage and began an opening soliloquy than he would be greeted by a wall of verbal abuse, heckles, so called witty comments and a barrage of rotting vegetables. It is said that the cook of The Artichoke was able to make one of the finest broths in all England from the rotting vegetable matter that was thrown at the stage every night.

During this period of history England pushed out its boundaries and expanded its trade. New discoveries were being made every day and map makers were being constantly kept busy by drawing and redrawing the newly discovered lands of the Americas. New continents meant new products and new consumer items for trade. Fortunes were waiting to be made. Many owners of York café-bars, in conjunction with the Merchant Adventurers, clubbed together to help finance the famous voyage of Sir Walter Raleigh. They invested heavily in this venture and were among the first in England to benefit from the new wonders that Raleigh brought back with him. Unfortunately, as they insisted on smoking the potatoes and making a strange tasting tea out of the tobacco, they very quickly went bankrupt .

Another famous resident of Elizabethan York was the so called mystic, sage, soothsayer, and fortune teller named Mother Boatweight. However, unlike Knaresborough's more famous Mother Shipton, nothing the York soothsayer ever said came true. Her followers lost great fortunes on the York races where, even if the horse was an odds-on, copper bottomed favourite running in a one horse race, if it was tipped by Mother Boatweight, it would lose. Eventually the owners of racehorses competing at York would pay Mother Boatweight large amounts of money not to mention their horses, and the racecourse owners paid her even more money to stay away all together.

Despite her bad record many people in York faithfully followed her advice, saying things like "you could never tell", and "it could be you" and hoping against hope that one day she might be proved right. However their attitudes radically changed after they all took her advice and put their shirts on Shergar to win the Magnet Gold Cup. Unfortunately on the night before the race the horse was spirited away by the fairies and was never seen again. As everyone in the town had put large ante-post bets on they lost the lot and they turned against the fortune teller with a vengeance.

The unfortunate woman was thrown into the river and, as she didn't sink, was pronounced mad and driven from the city by the angry citizens, who as well as waving losing betting slips in her face, told her that she should have seen it coming. Escaping with her life she made her way to London, changed her name to Meg, began wearing heavy make up and turned up some months later making equally ridiculous predictions on the National Lottery. Some other of Mother Boatweight's famous but unfortunate predictions stated that-

"In the reign of the Venerable Terry,
York Citie would win the F.A. Cup...........

A group of travelling York troubadours
would name themselves after a potato
depot and make many successful hit singles.....

When the luminary pumpkin crosses the
stellar track of the great peewit, York will
turn to chocolate...

A horse will become ruler of England
and weasels will inherit the earth."

Outside York, in the larger world, Elizabeth I had been busy flexing her power and surviving religious based plots and counter plots. The Catholic Mary Stuart, Queen of Scots, was still the heir to the throne and many Catholics saw the assassination of Elizabeth as an expedient way in which they could assure that a Catholic sympathiser would sit on the English throne once again.

Throughout this period many Catholics were executed for no other reason than trying to worship in their own faith. Laws were passed that made the holding or attendance of a Catholic Mass a punishable act, as was being a Catholic priest or harbouring and sheltering a priest. As a result of these draconian laws many people were hanged on York's infamous Tyburn situated on the Knavesmire by the Leeds road.

However the fate of Margaret Clitheroe, York's most famous Catholic Martyr, was to suffer a much more unpleasant and gruesome death. This woman, born in 1556 was married to a butcher when she was aged 15. She lived above their shop in The Shambles, where she converted an upstairs room into a secret room for hiding travelling priests. In 1586 she was caught and tried at York Assizes.

She refused to acknowledge the power of the court and refused to plead either guilty or not guilty. In such cases English law decreed *"peine forte et dure"*, which is nice pleasant lawyer speak meaning that the person on trial was to be sentenced to be pressed to death. Now this sort of death wasn't very nice, (actually when you stop to think about it no death really is!). It wasn't easy and it wasn't quick. In York's prison, situated on the end of Ouse Bridge, the poor woman was laid on the stone floor with a large stone positioned in the centre of her back. Then a large and very solid wooden door was placed on top of her and, at regular intervals, large weights were placed on the door which slowly crushed the life out of her. Margaret Clitheroe was cannonised in 1970 and a house in the Shambles was dedicated as a shrine to her memory. Today many people walking down the Shambles pop inside this building to reflect quietly in its atmospheric peace and calm. It's just a tad unfortunate that the shrine isn't actually in the house where Margaret lived. That house is further up the street.

Meanwhile back in the Elizabethan court, despite many attempts to implicate her in other plots, the anti-Catholic law makers eventually managed to stitch Mary up in something called The Babington Plot. She was imprisoned in Fotheringay castle and, in 1587, executed.

The following year, angered by the English supremacy of the sea routes between Europe and the New World, and by Elizabeth's so called heresy, King Philip II of Spain had a bit of a brainstorm. He decided to invade England! He amassed a large fleet of galleons with the intention of sailing up the English Channel to the Netherlands where he would pick up a large Spanish army and transport them all to the shores of England.

As soon as they got word of this great fleet sailing up the Channel, the English sea captains stopped playing bowls and set out in a number of small ships to harry the larger force and attacked them with fire ships. These attacks disrupted the great fleet so much that it broke up in disarray. Then, in what can only be described as an act of God, they got hit by a great storm, which disrupted them even more! The Armada was destroyed, Britannia once again ruled the waves, and wrecked Spanish ships appeared all over the British coast line.

It has been claimed by many historians that Elizabeth disliked any thought of her succession, taking the opinion, quiet rightly, that it was nothing to do with her! After the execution of Mary the rightful claimant to the English throne was Mary's son, James VI of Scotland and, in 1602 Robert Cecil, Elizabeth's Secretary of State, began to negotiate with James to assure a peaceful succession. It was just as well as, on 24th March 1603, Elizabeth died and James VI of Scotland became James I of England.

The news took three days to reach York by which time James VI or I (depending whether you were English or Scottish), was already packing his cases. On his way South he popped into York, staying the night at King's Manor where, in recognition of him being the first King James ever to stay in the city, the city fathers presented him with a sliver cup. Thus founding a peculiar English tradition that still applies today. Whether it is for playing pub darts in a minor northern league, exhibiting the biggest marrow in a garden fete, winning an egg and spoon race at the school sports day, or for winning the F.A. Cup Final, anyone who is first at anything always gets to win a silver cup.

When James I eventually arrived in London he found himself facing four problems - undercover Catholicism, increasing Puritanism, a moody House of Commons, and troubles abroad. He managed to solve the last one first by seeking reconciliation and securing peace with Spain. But the actions of the undercover Catholics resulted in one of the most infamous dates in the British calendar, as in "Remember, remember the 5th of November gunpowder treason and plot......"

The Gunpowder Plot was brought about by Catholic dissidents who had looked to James to create a more tolerant atmosphere to their faith. However they were bitterly disappointed. As soon as he became King, James he imposed more anti-Catholic laws. The Catholic cause now became desperate and, led by Thomas Winter and Robert Catsby, a plot to blow up both the King and the House of Lords was hatched.

The idea behind this action went as follows. If they destroyed the King as he was opening a new session of Parliament they would not only kill him, but also the Prince of Wales, and all the leading ministers. In the ensuing confusion they would seize the next in line to the throne, the five year old Prince Charles, and raise a general revolt. Then, governing in the young prince's name they would be able to restore Catholicism to England.

By the end of 1604 the plot was gaining strength. The plotters had recruited Thomas Percy and one Guy Fawkes, an explosive expert who had been fighting as a mercenary in Flanders. Using his influential connections Percy rented a cellar under the Houses of Parliament and by Feb. 1605 the plot was ready. However the planned meeting of Parliament was postponed until the following autumn. Despite the growing risk of discovery the original plotters gathered more followers until by October thirteen men were involved.

Then, just as they were poised to strike, they made the fatal mistake of showing a bit of pity. They tried to warn some of their Catholic friends and relatives that would be present. Lord Mounteagle received an anonymous letter asking him not to attend Parliament, but, instead of retiring to the country as advised, he passed the letter onto The Privy Seal who dispatched the Earl of Suffolk, Lord Chamberlain to investigate. At 11.00pm on the night of November 4th the Earl and his guard marched through the building with the express intent of checking out one particular cellar, owned by Thomas Percy. He found the cellar, guarded by a manservant named John Johnson, filled to the brim with coal and firewood. Johnson was arrested and the cellar searched. Underneath all the wood and coal they found thirty six barrels of gunpowder, each one fitted with a short fuse.

Johnson was immediately taken to the Tower where, under torture, he confessed that his real name was Guido Fawkes and implicated the other plotters. Catsby and Winter, along with seven companions, fled to the Midlands but were tracked down to Holbeach House in Staffordshire by The Sheriff of Worcestershire. On the morning of November 8th the Sheriff stormed the house and in the ensuing fracas four of the plotters were killed "resisting arrest". Winter, his brother and the other surviving conspirators were captured alive and brought back to London to face trail with Fawkes. It was no great surprise that they were found guilty and sentenced to be hanged, drawn and quartered. Not the most pleasant way to shuffle off this mortal coil.

Instead of helping, this failed plot severely damaged the Catholic cause. It was over two hundred years before the Catholics would re-establish their good name and gain full legal tolerance - despite the many more recent claims that Guy Fawkes was the only bloke that ever went into Parliament with the right intentions.

With true British respect for tradition this event became a yearly celebration - Bonfire Night. The night of the year when no piece of discarded furniture, fence post or garden gate is safe from fiery destruction. The night in which thousands of hard earned British pounds are squandered in the purchase of cheap Chinese made fireworks that blow the bollocks off anyone foolish enough to stand within a hundred feet of them. Even today in our age of microchips and information super highways, it is still traditional to make something that resembles a human shape out of bits of old clothing, stick a mask on it and send children dragging it round the streets begging for "a penny for the Guy".

Traditional foods such as parkin and treacle toffee are also prepared to be served around the bonfire. However in more recent times these have been replaced by blackened, half raw sausages, and potatoes especially cooked to be red hot on the outside and stone cold in the middle.

Now why is all this Gunpowder Plot stuff here in this book of York's history I hear you ask? Well York just happened to be the birthplace of Guido "the poor fella who was caught in the cellar" Fawkes.

Although the precise location of his birth is not known, records show that he was baptised at the church of St. Michael-Le-Belfry on 16th April 1570 and was educated at St. Peter's School. His father died when he was ten, and his stepfather was a staunch Roman Catholic. Due to his influence most of his friends and his school teacher were also Catholic sympathisers. An interesting aside is that along with Fawkes another four of the gunpowder plotters were also old boys of St. Peter's School. I can't help wondering if they celebrate bonfire night, and if so how? How Fawkes came to be a mercenary explosives expert fighting for Spain in Flanders is another story and one that shows the wide availability and successes of the Elizabethan job creation schemes.

From 1600 to 1630 the population of York grew to 12,000 and it was still the second city in the land. But the place was still damp, dark, dangerous and squalid with an unsatisfactory water supply and a very bad smell that drifted up from the river to combine with the odour from the many piggeries and street refuse. This smell must have assaulted the nose with the power of a large cricket bat. It must have been ten times worse than the present day nasty smell that emanates from the sugar factory on Boroughbridge Road that, on bad wind days, drifts across the city causing tourists to wrinkle their noses and look around for something that just crept up behind them and died.

It was these insanitary conditions that, despite attempts to clean up the city, caused the outbreaks of two more plagues. One in 1604 and another in 1631. An example of just how unhealthy the city was can be gathered by a court report from 1607 when one George Hobson, resident of Stonegate, was put away for three months because -

"about a month since he cast filth out of a pott forth of a Chamber window in his house into the Strete on the daie tyme which lyght on the heades of certain countrie men who were filling their waynes at the said widow Waslinge dore.... some whereof did lyght on the said widow Waslinge."

Apparently the words *"some whereof"* is polite lawyer speak literally meaning a crock full of shit! Mind you today this action wouldn't be seen so much as a crime but more like slapstick comedy.

Over the years Ouse Bridge had expanded and had become overcrowded with various shops and buildings. At one end was the Sheriffs Goal and the other St. William's Chapel. These were linked by twenty three shops on the north side and another twenty nine on the south. The most famous of these shops were Mr Floppie's Olde English Pie and Figgy Pudding Shoppe, Arnold Bumstitcher's Trouser and Legging Shoppe, Peter Panting's Bassoon, Woodwind and Second-hande Wurdle Emporium, and Mrs Figgin's Outsize Ladies Fashions for Fashionable Outsize Ladies. There were also a number of ye olde souvenir and trinket shoppes as well as some residential houses. It was business as normal until one fateful day in 1568 when, due to a sudden thaw, the river rose and the swollen waters washed away two of the bridge's central supporting arches. Twelve houses fell into the river and twelve people drowned.

At least that was the official story. If you begin to dig around in the archives a slightly different story comes to light. It seems that a year before the bridge collapsed the City Council agreed -

"that the reparation of Ousebridge in masonrie
shall with all convenient spede be sett apon"

Suitable stones from the ruined chapels of Foss Bridge and from the Holy Trinity Priory in Micklegate were found and set aside for the job. Three months later, on examining the projected budget, the council decided to appoint someone else to examine the existing bridge and -

"if therapon they can perceyve that it will hold and contynew still as it is without great jeopardy then the sayd worke to stay unto an other tyme."

It comes as no great surprise to discover that these so called council paid experts declared that the bridge was perfectly safe and would stand for many years to come - it collapsed within the year.

As at that time Ouse Bridge was the only way of getting from one side of the city to the other, its collapse proved a bit of a problem. Robert Maskewe and John Wilkynson were granted the right of operating a replacement ferry on the condition that *"all franchised men inhabityng within this citie"* were given free passage for themselves and their horses and carriages whilst *"strangers or foreyners"* had to pay one penny for a man and his horse, and a halfpenny for a footman alone, return, not transferable.

It took two years of arguments about the responsibility of who should pay the cost and fund the finance before the bridge was rebuilt. At first the civic fathers ordered the parish constables to bring them lists of every householder who would be willing to give money towards the cost of rebuilding the bridge. This job didn't take too long as it soon became very apparent that no one would willingly put their hand in their pockets. The civic fathers rethought their strategy and, surprise surprise, came up with the idea of levying a form of council tax. Every household was assessed and the levy was payable in four equal parts on the 25th of May, June, July & August. Eventually after seeking yet more expert advice and bringing in outside expertise from London the building of the new bridge commenced in April 1564.

When it was finished it was one of the wonders of the city. It now had five arches, the central one being 81 feet wide and 17 feet high. It still housed a number of buildings including the surviving houses, a new Sunday School, law courts, a prison and a new council chamber housed in St. William's Chapel.

Around this period the first ever map of York was made by the famous map maker John Speed. It could be found as an insert in a larger map of the West Riding of Yorkshire. On close examination with a magnifying glass it shows the city still surrounded by the ancient stone walls. Streets such as The Shambles, Petergate, Walmgate can be clearly identified, but what is surprising are the large number of windmills in the city. If anyone bothers to find a copy of this map and count them all they will find that Speed drew fifteen of them. There are no prizes for guessing why they were needed and it wasn't due to the Elizabethans suddenly becoming environmentally aware. In fact it was due to exactly the opposite. The river, what with silting up and being filled to the brim with the sewage and garbage of the city, just didn't flow fast enough to drive as many mills as the city needed and so wind power was used.

On the outskirts of York on a slight hill in the leafy suburb of Acomb one of these windmills is still standing. Originally it was owned by a miller who went by the name of Windy and who made a living grinding corn and wheat for the local bakers. In the great storm of 1602 the windmill caught fire and it was only due to the quick response and heroics of the local fire militia led by three Acomb citizens named Drew, Drew and Barny McGrew, that the building was saved.

Meanwhile James I continued to rule and continued to get up the nose of Parliament. The situation wasn't made any better by the attitude of the King himself. James I thought himself a learned man, indeed before he moved south he had written and published a treatise on the "True Law of Free Monarchies", claiming that "Kings are breathing images of God upon earth". England had experienced many rulers throughout its history and many people remembered stories from the past that instead of seeming to be the "image of God on earth" made kings seem more like power crazed, blood letting loonies and money grabbing tyrants.

Not satisfied with writing and publishing his daft ideas James also took to lecturing Parliament and his Justices on his theories of the supernatural powers of kings. Eventually everyone became thoroughly fed up with this constant theorising and lecturing and Parliament began to develop some theories of their own.

James was succeeded by his son in 1625. Charles I was only twenty four when he became king. He had experienced a very sheltered upbringing, learning from the writings and teachings of his father and to Parliament there seemed no break in continuity. The new King even used the same advisers as his father, so it was no great surprise that he fell out with Parliament as soon as he began his reign and, from 1629 to 1640, he tried ruling the country without them. He revived old outdated methods of taxation and then really upset everyone when in 1635 and 1636 he altered the rules to an existing shipping tax. Up to now this tax was payable by ports and went to pay for the building of warships. Suddenly Charles moved the goal posts so that all counties had to pay this tax, whether they had ports or not. You can well imagine the happiness that broke out in such landlocked counties as Rutland and Nottinghamshire!

As well as creating problems and upsetting people in the country with his own taxation policies, Charles employed other advisors who managed to drop him deeper into the mire. His chief state and church advisors were Archbishop Laud and the Earl of Stafford, Thomas Wentworth. Between them they planned to establish a system of autocratic monarchic government and re-introduce ceremonies in religious observation. Archbishop Laud even tried to introduce a new prayer book. In an action that would be repeated by the Tory government of the late 1980's, they tried experimenting by testing out their new policies in Scotland. Just like the actions of the Scots some three hundred years later, the nation revolted. They raised an army and attacked England, first in 1639 and again in 1640. Charles needed to quell this revolt, and needed an army, but in order to raise an army he needed to increase his revenue through taxation, and in order to do that he needed to placate the very Parliament that he thought he could do without.

In order to help these delicate negotiations and to establish a bargaining position, Charles had to ditch both Archbishop Laud and Thomas Wentworth. The latter was tried under a Bill of Attainer, found guilty and executed in 1641. Thus teaching all students of history a very salutary lesson. To wit, it's all right having friends in high places, but when the proverbial whatsit hits the fan you're usually on your own.

Charles returned quickly to York and made the town centre of his operations. Not trusting anyone he left behind in London he brought with him the Royal Mint, establishing it in Mint Yard, near Bootham Bar.

Charles put his foot down and refused to budge when Parliament demanded reforms in the Church of England and the right to control the militia, the only armed force in the Kingdom with the exception of the royal bodyguard. This demand brought out the worst in Charles and in a fit of petulance in 1642, he attempted a royal *coup d'etat.* He entered the House Of Commons and attempted to arrest five leading members of the opposition, but he was too late, they had already escaped. The failure of this Royal coup brought the country to the brink of Civil War.

Charles had visited York twice prior to the outbreak of war. Once in 1633 on a long-break, have-it-away weekend break which he spent at King's Manor. He must have been incredibly bored during his visit because whilst he was there he borrowed a Swiss army pen knife from the concierge and slowly and methodically carved his initials on the front of the building where they can still be seen today.

In 1639 he came back for a month when he "kept his Maundy", that quaint and truly English tradition when the reigning monarch gives the same number of old age pensioners as the years of his age new gowns, a free shirt each, shoes and stockings, one purse containing twenty pence and another containing thirty nine single pennies, and a wooden platter complete with salt, fish, a loaf and finally to help the wash it all down, a cup of wine. Just the job.

When they stopped bowing and curtsying enough to wave him a very grateful good-bye the old age pensioners of York had no idea that they would be seeing Charles I return to the City as quickly as he did.

CHAPTER TEN

THE ENGLISH CIVIL WAR.

As Civil War finally broke out Charles returned to York, this time bringing with him his own printing press which he established in St. William's College. As by now he wasn't very popular in London, he made desperate attempts to make York his new capital city, and in June 1642, he summoned the nobility and gentry of Yorkshire to a large open air meeting held on Heworth Moor. Always interested to see what the King was up to next, a vast curious crowd gathered.

Unfortunately this crowd wasn't half as friendly as the King had hoped, indeed as many of them held the totally opposite point of view, they were not very friendly to him at all. One of these was a Yorkshire land owner called Sir Thomas Fairfax who, as a moderate and reasonable sort of man, wanted to reach some sort of understanding with the King. To this end he, along with many of his supporters, had drawn up a petition stating their disagreements with Royal Policies and offering a suitable compromise. Sir Thomas had volunteered to give this petition to the King in person, and so made his way to Heworth Moor. However, when he arrived he found Heworth Moor a very crowded place. Ever eager to sell their various wares, many York traders had set up various stalls and entertainment booths, and the crowds were surrounded by fast food stands, ale stalls, tell-your- fortune stalls, guess the weight of the pig competitions, and all the general melee and confusion of an average 17th century fun fair.

Stopping only to taste the dubious delights of Arthyur Goolies original Vole Pie, "a bit like a pork pie but only smaller", Sir Thomas eventually forced his way through the crowd and managed to get alongside the King.

It was then that one of life's little ironies suddenly squeezed itself out of the bottom of fate and dropped firmly to the ground on Heworth Moor.

Just as he was about to present his petition, the King's horse reared suddenly, knocking Sir Thomas off his feet, and almost trampling him into the earth in the process. Despite the King later claiming it was an accident, the general feeling of the crowd was that Charles had attempted to ride Sir Thomas down. The unfortunate gent was picked up, brushed down, declared a popular hero and given a quart of Nut Brown Ale for his troubles,

The upshot of this unfortunate incident was that Charles realised he wasn't as popular in York as he thought he was and promptly left. He marched to Nottingham where he raised his Royal Standard thus giving the official sign that Civil War had finally kicked off.

By now, and irrespective of the King's personal popularity, the City of York had been turned into the northern Royalist headquarters. Its commander in chief was The Earl of Cumberland who suddenly got landed with the job of making York defensible. Lucky him! His first job was to attempt to restore Clifford's Tower. As the building had been sold off to a private citizen in 1613, he first had to make arrangements to rent the property back from the new owners before strengthening the floors and building a new front on it. Cumberland was nicely getting on with things when he was suddenly replaced by the more energetic Earl of Newcastle who promptly hired a number of labourers to dig a series of defensive earthworks around the castle. A 17th century writer noted that -

> *"....the Citie was everywhere strongly*
> *fortified, and above twenty cannon,*
> *great and small were planted around*
> *it. Two cannon were planted on Baile Hill,*
> *two at Micklegate bar, two at Monk Bar,*
> *two at Walmgate Bar out of which last*
> *was a strong bulwark erected.*
>
> *At several lanes ends, within the cityies*
> *walls, were ditches and banks made and*
> *cast up, with hogsheads filled with earth*
> *for barracadoes. By the Generals orders*

the magistrates were to find eight hundred men to work daily at the repairs of the walls, and securing the ditches of the city."

Bloody typical isn't it, the King and Parliament declare war on each other and who gets to do all the digging? The poor working class people of York! Mind you the overtime was good, and for once there was no unemployment In fact when people arrived to sign on, the bloke at the Benefits Agency just handed them a pick and a shovel and told them to get on with it.

On 1st January 1644 the Scots, who were spoiling for a fight anyway and had allied themselves with Parliament, marched into England with an army of over twenty thousand men. On hearing this news the Royalist Garrison of York, led by the Marquis of Newcastle set out to march north and face them. Meanwhile further south a small Yorkshire Parliamentary force commanded by Sir Thomas Fairfax and his father Lord Ferdinando Fairfax also planned to march north, only their objective was to assist the Scots by attacking the Royalist force from the rear.

Unfortunately a message bearing this news was intercepted and taken to York. The commander left in charge, a man named Bellasis, made a quick decision. He decided to march his force out from York to meet the Parliamentarians at Selby. Big mistake! - He was utterly defeated, a situation which left the City of York defenceless. On hearing the news the Marquis of Newcastle went ape shit. He had just spent the last few days marching his army north and had almost reached Durham, now, on hearing the news, he had to turn them around and march back to York, and in double quick time before the Fairfaxes arrived and walked in through the open doors.

He made it, just. On 16th April he and his army entered the city and shut the gates behind them, right in the face of the Fairfaxes. Meanwhile the Scots army, realising that the Parliamentarians had turned round and gone back to York, decided to follow them. By the end of the week York found itself surrounded by two huge Parliamentary armies and the "Great Siege of York" began.

Despite their numbers, the Parliamentarians realised that they couldn't capture the city without reinforcements and asked Parliament for more troops. Subsequently the army of the Eastern Association commanded by the Earl of Manchester and whose second commander was a bloke called Oliver Cromwell was ordered to join the siege. They arrived on the 4th June and then city was completely surrounded.

As would be expected, many skirmishes occurred around the city and its occupants developed a habit of scurrying in and out of the small narrow mediaeval streets with their heads down, avoiding the hail of cannon balls, small shot, and other dangerous missiles that constantly rained down on them. The main target was the Castle and its garrison, and the people living nearby soon found a hundred and one reasons why they should visit and move in with relatives who lived in the opposite side of the city.

The houses that were situated outside the City walls created many problems for the defenders. Mostly these were uninhabited, with the residents safely behind the city walls, but the deserted houses gave shelter for the many snipers and miners that were with the besieging army. Hence, every so often, and usually under cover of darkness, Royalists would sneak out from the safety of the city walls and try to pull down and demolish the empty houses. Despite these defensive tactics the Parliamentary miners managed to dig tunnels towards the city in two different places. Fairfax's men tunnelled towards Walmgate Bar whilst Manchester's men tunnelled under St. Mary's Tower, near to Bootham Bar.

The Walmgate tunnel was quickly discovered. The Royalists dug a hole above it and flooded it with water, making it useless, but they never discovered the one under St. Mary's until it was too late.

On 16th June, Trinity Sunday, whilst many of the defenders were attending Matins in the Minster, the Parliamentarians exploded their mine under St. Mary's Tower. It went off with a bloody great bang, destroying some of the tower and the nearby wall and showering a huge pile of stone and soil all over the City. As the dust cleared over six hundred men armed with scaling ladders poured into the breach. They ran through the hole in the wall and made it as far as the gardens and orchards of Kings Manor before the defenders arrived and rallied a counter attack. Other defenders ran through Lendal Postern, up the river bank and then up Marygate, effectively cutting the attackers off from their own lines. After a lot of serious hand-to-hand fighting the defenders managed to beat off the attack and over three hundred Parliamentarians troops were killed or captured.

After the failed attack things calmed down a bit whilst everyone took stock. The occupants of the city continued to keep their heads down and the besiegers settled back and contended themselves with firing cannons and taking pot shots at anything that moved above or beyond the city walls.

Throughout the siege conditions on the outside of the City were almost as bad as conditions on the inside. The size of the besieging army created great hygiene problems for the attackers. Lets face it, the only public toilets for miles around were within the city, behind the fortified walls. It must be remembered, that these were pre-chemical toilet days and that we are talking about a period before the invention of that unique piece of equipment found at most of today's outdoor events - the Portaloo.

As anyone who has ever been to a three or four day festival, such as Glastonbury or Reading, knows the most important item of anyone's survival kit is a spare loo roll. No matter how wet or muddy the camp site becomes, no matter how bad the acts are, no matter the length of the queue at the beer tent, the greatest luxury of outdoor camping life is the ability to wipe ones bottom with something like a sheet or two of Andrex double soft extra texture.

Unfortunately loo paper had not really caught on at this point in time and all around the City of York plants with wide leaves became a premium. Rhubarb was favorite, its large leaves almost going as far as a small loo roll. When the rhubarb ran out it was down to the leaves of the dock plant. From there it was down to grass and mosses. From there on you were on your own. Soon there wasn't a plant with leaves for miles around - with the exception of the nettles and thistles. One unfortunate attacker, in desperation, did try nettles but his screams were so blood curdling that the besiegers thought they were being attacked by another force. This confusion lasted as long as it took the guard to find the screaming man trying to lower his bare and very lumpy red bottom into the cooling waters of the River Ouse.

Food in the besiegers camp was also at a premium. Knowing this fact the more enterprising of the local purveyors of take-away foods set up a roaring trade. Every night, under cover of darkness, a host of small movable stalls and men carrying trays of hot meat pies would sneak out of the city to ply their wares among the enemy armies. As camp cookery was pretty fundamental and the besiegers had eaten everything it was possible to eat for miles around the arrival of hot take away food stuffs was like manna from heaven.

The food stuff smelt so good and the army was so hungry that no one bothered to think as to where all this food was actually coming from. After all the city had been cut off from the outside world for some time and no fresh supplies were arriving. Whilst there are no existing records of the menus we can gain a clue as to what was actually in the pies and burgers by the fact that the following year York Council were forced to make a few people redundant due to lack of work. These people were the four city dog wardens, and all the towns rat catchers.

Realising what was going on the Royalists came to an agreement with the food sellers. The Royalists would be allowed to add a certain something to the food and the food sellers wouldn't be shot for treason. Survival being the name of the game the deal sounded fair enough to the food sellers, and so one day a special concoction was developed that involved a mixture of mince meat, spices such as chilies and curry power, senna pods, liquorice and cod liver oil, all blended together with a nice dressing of spinach marinated in turpentine.

Later that night, sometime after the food sellers had returned, the citizens of York were awoken from their beds by a strange noise that sounded like 30,000 men all moaning together at the same time. No sooner had the citizens stuck their heads out of their bedroom windows to find out what was going on when it seemed that the city was suddenly struck by a mighty thunderstorm, only there was no rain or lightening. Then the smell hit them. The York residents quickly slammed their windows shut, stuffed carpets under the gaps beneath their doors, dived into bed and pulled the covers over their heads, and stayed there until they were sure it had gone away. As a result of this evil nights work a bout of sickness swept through the besieging army and it was with some relief (no pun intended!) that the news reached them that Prince Rupert was at Knaresborough on his way to attack them.

The Parliamentarians figured that Prince Rupert would march straight to the city along the A59 Harrogate to York road, and lifted the siege to gather their forces to the west of the river in the small villages of Long Marston, Hessay and Tockwith where, on the morning of 1st July, they lined up in battle formation on nearby Marston Moor.

But Prince Rupert had a trick up his sleeve. He sent a detachment of cavalry to seize Skip Bridge that crossed the Nidd, thus misleading the Parliamentarian generals into thinking it was his advanced guard. Instead he marched the rest of his army north via Boroughbridge to cross the Ure, on to Thornton Bridge to cross the Swale, and down the east bank of the Ouse arriving in the Clifton and Skelton areas of York on the night of 1st of July. The Prince never entered into York, instead he sent his second in command, General George Goring, into the city to give his compliments to the Marquis of Newcastle and tell him to have his men ready to march out by four in the morning. It didn't come as a great surprise to Prince Rupert that by quarter past four the Marquis and his men still hadn't arrived. Not wishing to lose the element of surprise he marched his own force on to Marston Moor.

Meanwhile having waited on Marston Moor for an entire day and not seeing hide nor hair of the Royalist army, the Parliamentarians figured that they must have moved south to cross the river at either Selby or Tadcaster. As dawn broke on 2nd of July, just as Prince Rupert was leaving York, the Parliamentarian army packed their bags and began to move south towards Tadcaster, leaving behind some three thousand cavalry who sat on the top of a small rise and watched with disbelief as a large Royalist force began to build up in front of them as behind them their own infantry was managing to string itself out in a long line that stretched between Tadcaster and Tockwith.

Messengers on fast horses were sent out to carry the news for them to turn back, which must have been really good news for the front part of the army that had already reached Tadcaster by the time the horsemen caught up with them. I would love to have heard the comments that were murmured under their collective breaths when they were told to turn around, march all the way back to Marston Moor, and then fight a battle. It can safely be assumed that the intelligence and legitimacy of their officers was severely questioned all the way back during the long walk.

Mind you if confusion was gaining the upper hand among the Parliamentarians it was beginning to run amok among the Royalists. Despite Prince Rupert's request for the Marquis to turn up at four o'clock the man didn't bother showing his face until after breakfast. Finally, when he did show up around nine, he strolled onto Marston Moor accompanied only by his personal staff, having left his force back in York. History records the words of Prince Rupert as being -

"My Lord I wish you had come sooner with your forces."

Personally I very much doubt the accuracy of that report! I have a feeling that a man seeing his advantage of surprise slip from his grasp by someone not obeying orders, and faced with the same bloke strolling along four hours later with his hands in his pockets, his pipe in his mouth and his army still in York, would probably have said something slightly more colourful. Something along the lines of "What the &£%$ do you think you're $£!%&*% doing, you *&%$£!* son of a !"%£*. Now why don't you turn right around, stuff your pipe up your arse, go back to York and bring your &^%$£!&* army back with you this time!"

For most of the day Rupert, paced, fretted and generally pulled his hair out as he watched the Parliamentary army build up once again as he waited for Newcastle's forces to turn up. It was four o'clock in the afternoon when they finally took their battle positions, only a mere twelve hours late.

The two sides organised themselves and reorganised themselves, until early evening. Around seven o'clock Rupert decided there wouldn't be battle that day after all and went off to have his supper in his tent at the rear of the field. The Marquis of Newcastle is said to have returned to his private coach to smoke yet another pipe! (I think it's a fair question to ask just what was it in the pipe that he was smoking!)

As the Royalists enjoyed a bit of relaxation, a sudden thunderstorm broke out and under cover of the thunder and lightening the Parliamentarians began to advance and the battle finally kicked off with it's front line stretching almost two and a half miles, between the villages of Tockwith and Long Marston.

By ten o'clock it was all over. During the long and bloody three hours of fighting the Royalists were routed, over 4,000 were killed and another 1,500 taken prisoner, whilst the Parliamentarian forces suffered the loss of only 300. Rupert fled back to York where the following morning he met with Newcastle. This time history records that *"warme words"* were exchanged between the two men. They must have been very *"warme words"* indeed for after their meeting Rupert left the City heading for Richmond whilst Newcastle headed towards Scarborough, caught the next boat for Hamburg, and stayed there until the Restoration some years later.

The York Garrison finally surrendered on 16th July and the agreed terms of surrender allowed the defenders to march out of the city with their arms, flying their colours, and beating their drums. They were allowed to travel as far as Skipton without harm.

Only after Royalists had left did the Parliamentarian leaders entered into the city. They went straight to the Minster where they held a service of thanksgiving whilst the rest of the towns occupants got on with their every-day business. The builders of the town grabbed the opportunity with both hands and were soon seen scurrying around with tape measures and competitive quotations for rebuilding the bits of the city that "Cromwell had knocked around a bit".

An unfortunate casualty of the siege was a York man named Matthew Floppie, the owner of a small hot pie stall. Along with many other traders he frequently snuck out of the city in order to sell his Hot Meat Pies to the besieging army of Roundheads and Scots. Unfortunately, on the night of July 1st, he tried to sell a hot chicken and mushroom pie to Prince Rupert as he led the Royalist Army to lift the siege. He was put to death on the spot by an over enthusiastic cavalier who knew very well the Princes' irrational fear of chickens, alive or in pies. However as some sort of industrial compensation his wife was given the pie concession for the following day's Battle Of Marston Moor.

The night before the battle she went to work calling in many helpers and assistants until as dawn broke she had amassed a number of tasty pies, peas, snacks and other delicacies. These she put onto the back of a covered wagon and drove it out of the city, through Acomb, over the ring road and down to Marston Moor through Rufforth. As she arrived in Long Marston she noticed that to her left the Parliamentarians were beginning to wander away, whilst to her right the Royalist army was starting to build up. Taking her courage in both hands she stopped on the outskirts of Tockwith and erected her small canvas booth from which she hung two freshly painted signs. On the Royalist side she hung the sign that read "Pies fit for a Prince." and on the Parliamentarian side she hung another sign that read "Pies for the People." Throughout the entire day she did a roaring trade, and was just about to pack up when a thunderstorm broke. The next thing she knew she was in the middle of a Parliamentary cavalry charge. Being the wife of pie seller and coming from a long line of fearless York pie sellers she stood her ground and watched as the mounted men charged by. Indeed this brave woman stood her ground throughout the following three hours still serving hot snacks as cannon balls dropped all around her.

It is even recorded that, at the height of the battle, the entire regiment of The Duke of Monmouth's Tenth Foot and Mouth Brigade called a special "time out" in order to eat her delicious hot steak and kidneys. Indeed in later years Cromwell himself stated that the

Roundheads wouldn't have won the battle if they hadn't been fortified by Mrs Floppie's Pies and Mushy Peas.

Today on a little used road leading from the village of Long Marston to Tockwith there is a large stone memorial that marks the site of the battlefield complete with little diagrams to show where everyone was when the battle started. It is to the eternal shame of the designers that they omitted the site of Mrs Floppies pie stall.

Many ghostly sightings have been claimed to have been seen in the surrounding area, usually involving sightings of various stragglers and survivors of the battle. However it has to be remembered that, at various times of the year, members from the quasi-military organisation The Sealed Knot, and the other, less military based organisation The English Civil War Society, dress up as Cavaliers and Roundheads and wander around the area scaring the local children.

Every year, on the actual anniversary of the battle, the Sealed Knot, watched by members of The English Civil War Society, hold a ceremony around this monument. With great ceremony and watched by two disinterested traffic policemen, they pull a reproduction cannon along the road from Tockwith and fire it over the site, before marching up and down the road again beating a big drum. If you look very carefully at this procession there is always a representative of S.H.E.P.A.M.P. (The Society of Historic English Pies and Mushy Peas) walking behind the parade carrying a tray full of historically accurate reproductions of 17th century pies and not so hot mushy peas.

The loss of York was a severe blow to the Royalist cause. After the lifting of the siege Sir Thomas Fairfax besieged Helmsley which he eventually captured before being appointed Commander in Chief of "The New Model Army" - which he led to victory at Naseby, the last major battle of the Civil War. Fairfax had now become one of the most important men in the country and for the next three years led the delicate negotiations between the King, the Scots, Parliament, and the Army.

In 1646 King Charles fled from Oxford and sought refuge with the Scots. After many long, tedious meetings and arguments they eventually agreed to hand him over to Parliament for the sum of £400,000, cash. Half up front, the rest over a course of time. It was then agreed that York would be the place where the money should be handed over.

This huge amount of cash arrived in the city in 1647, packed into over two hundred barrels and was held for safety in the Guildhall. When the Scots arrived, much to everyone's surprise, they insisted on counting it all - every penny. It is believed that this action is the source for the traditional English line of thought that claims that all Scots are tight fisted. This is not true, they are just very careful with their money, especially when it comes to dealing with English governments. It is said that the barrels contained so much loose change that it took the auditors twelve days to count it all, whilst the Scots had a twelve day, all expenses paid, free holiday in the City.

When it was finally agreed that all the money was there King Charles was handed over, taken to London and eventually brought to trial at Westminster Hall on 27th January. He was executed three days later on a specially constructed scaffold built in the Palace of Westminster.

To the very end the King was accompanied by a York man, Sir Thomas Herbert who had been born in 1606 into a wealthy merchant York family who owned a house on Pavement. The 17th century building known as Herbert House, now a tastefully reproduced Pizza house, built in 1616 now stands on the site. When Civil War broke out Herbert supported Parliament, and when the King was imprisoned in Holmby House in 1647, Herbert was sent by Parliament to act as a personal servant, with strict instructions to keep his eye on him. Despite their opposing viewpoints the two men formed a short friendship and so it was that Herbert accompanied the King to the executioner's block. As the King prepared to kneel he handed Herbert his watch and cloak. After the execution Herbert returned to York and lived at 9 High Petergate where he died in 1681.

York played little part in the period of the Commonwealth and Protectorate, but was poised to play an important part in the Restoration. Cromwell died in 1658 (his death mask can be seen in York's Castle Museum, although how they got their hands on it goodness only knows), and was succeeded by his son Richard, who abdicated a few months later.

Chapter Eleven

The Restoration

Once again historians tell us that "popular opinion" favoured the return of the Stuart monarchy. How this popular opinion was actually gauged is not known, especially when you consider that such things as MORI and exit polls were not yet invented.

Anyway, in Scotland, General Monk commander of 7,000 Parliamentarian troops figured it was time for a change and so he marched his army south only to find his progress barred by 10,000 troops commanded by General Lambert. In order to prevent bloodshed and the intervention of general mayhem, advice was sought from Thomas Fairfax who was living just outside York at Nun Appleton. Fairfax promised his support and in January 1660 marched onto the familiar ground of Marston Moor where he met with Lambert. The two generals decided to talk things over and Fairfax persuaded Lambert to join with him. They then allowed General Monk to enter York and for the next five days the three generals held a series of meetings inside the City to decided how to bring about the restoration of the Stuart monarchy.

At first the York residents, having long memories, must have felt slightly ill at ease seeing between 17,000 and 20,000 soldiers camped outside its walls. However when it became obvious that they were not about to siege the city, nor even fight each other, the more daring of the merchants and hot pie sellers saw a chance to make a killing. Mrs Floppie, still flushed with the success of her venture at Marston Moor, began to bake pies like she had never baked before. She doubled the number of people working for her and instigated a twenty four hour shift operation, turning out a wide variety of hot meat pies and even experimenting with a new culinary delight which she called a flan.

This experiment came about by accident when a young apprentice baker cooked a batch of pies and forgot to put the lids on them. However when Mrs Floppie put them on sale they proved to be a great success. Mainly because the purchasers could, for the first time, actually see what was in the pies! It had always been a very debatable point as to what meat Mrs Floppy had actually filled her pies with. Her marketing manager always claimed it was the finest cooking steak. Others claimed it was anything that walked, hopped or ran on four legs. Other less charitable people said it was anything that could actually slither! To this day no copies of her recipes have ever turned up, but it is worth noting that throughout this period her own records show payments paid to two of the towns public servants. The City dog catcher and the City rat catcher. It is also worth noting that throughout this period. residents noticed a remarkable lack of rabbits, stoats, weasels, frogs, newts and any other small creatures around the York area.

Anyway, back to the plot! After their meetings it was decided that Monk would continue his march south to summoned something called "The Rump", which was not, as some people think, a cut of meat, but the remains of Parliament. This group of politicians met and decided to restore the monarchy. They got a group of six peers and twelve commoners led by Thomas Fairfax to travel to Holland where the son of Charles I, called Charles (It's interesting to note that the monarchy still hadn't got the hang of originality in naming their children), was living in exile.

Charles was eventually persuaded to return to England via Dover. On his voyage he was accompanied by Samuel Pepys, the famous society diarist, who wrote for Hello magazine and other tabloids of the time. He wrote -

> *"On his first night at sea The King, upon the quarter-deck fell into discourse of his escape from Worcester, where it made me ready to weep to hear the stories he told of his difficulties.*
>
> *He was wearing a long brown cloak and underneath a shirt with a bold floral design. His boots were of the finest Spanish leather, and the addition of a simple feather in his hat band was a stroke of genius. I only*

suspect that this fashion will soon be sweeping the nation."

Pepys then continued to record who had designed the King's clothes, which of his friends were travelling with him, who the current female "court" favourite was and then made a number of very detailed remarks on the amount of cellulite that appeared around her thighs.

On 29th May Charles entered London riding a white horse given to him by Thomas Fairfax and bred at his stables at Nun Appleton. This gift was not very popular in York as, for weeks before, the York residents had been piling money on ante-post bets for the animal to win the coming Magnet Gold Cup. It is believed that this horse, if it hadn't been given away, would have won hands down. As it was, when it was withdrawn, the York residents took the only available option open to them for them to save their money. They hanged the bookie!

The Restoration of the monarchy was celebrated throughout England but especially in York where for a number of years now, the residents had learnt how to really party! Francis Drake, the historian not the sailor, described the celebrations as thus -

"York - May 11. The lord mayor, aldermen and twenty four, on horseback in their proper habits, preceded the cavalcade on foot in their gowns. These were attended by more than a thousand citizens under arms, and lastly came a troop of country gentlemen, near three hundred, with Lord Fairfax at their head, who all rode with their swords draw and hats upon their swords points.

When the proclamation was read at the usual places, the bells rung, the cannon played from the tower, and the soldiers gave several vollies of shot. At night were tar-barrles bonfires, illuminations, & all the pubs gave free entertainment. Aldo's Orphans, last seen playing during Queen Elizabeths time, reformed and played at an hostelry called "The Thatched Pig". Barry Garrett and his group of novelty lute players played at another inn called "The Spotted Thing", and Charlie Daykin publisher of pamphlets and leader of a group of musicians called "The Accidental Presbyterians" played at another venue called "Ye Olde Crossed Legs". The residents of the town spent their nights with the greatest of joy that could possibly be testified on that happy day. Especially as all drinks were free!"

The second son of Charles I was called James and on the restoration of Charles II James was made Duke of York. As Charles had no children, James was also heir to the throne. Among his many titles, James was Lord High Admiral of the British Navy and, in 1667, was responsible for sending a squadron of the fleet to America. This squadron captured the city of New Amsterdam from the Dutch and, in honour of James, the place was renamed New York. They would have called it New York, New York, but in those days it wasn't so much of "a hell'uv a town" as to warrant naming it twice, despite "the Bronx being up and the Battery down"!

The reign of Charles II, better known as the period of The Restoration, was a watershed in the history of Britain. Not only did it herald the dawning of a new period of gentrification - it also heralded great advances in the arts.

For the first time for ages the theatre was free of puritanical censorship, and writers such as Sir Thomas Killigrew and Sir William D'Avenant took full advantage. Killigrew ran the "Kings Company of Players", based at Drury Lane whilst D'Avenant, claiming to be William Shakespeare's illegitimate son, ran the "Duke of York's Company" at Lincoln's Inn Fields. As this period also coincided with the arrival of female actresses it seemed natural that playwrights would seize their opportunity to experiment in the more bawdy and licentious areas of writing. Let's face it, up to now all female roles had been played by young men so there hadn't been much point in writing in nude scenes. Suddenly the new plays hit a surprised public with the same effect as finding a buxom, topless, grinning "model" on page three of tomorrow's Daily Telegraph.

One of these actresses who "flaunted their wares" was the infamous Nell Gwynne who worked her way up from selling oranges outside Drury Lane to become a leading actress and from there straight into the King's bed. Who would have thought that orange retailing could lead to such exciting career prospects!

Leisure pursuits suddenly began to flourish, especially in the country areas where previously popular pastimes as hunting, wrestling, animal baiting, and a primitive form of football, were once again allowed. This primitive form of our national game usually took the form of a large, inter-village free-for-all, the object of which was seemingly to get a ball from one place to the other, whilst also smashing as many heads and kicking as many shins as possible. It has been said (but not by me!) that a certain similarity with that old fashioned style of football can still be found watching the home games at Bootham Crescent.

Fishing also became a popular hobby, especially after the publication of Isaak Walton's book "The Compleat Angler". Published in 1653, this book was one of the very first in a long and ponderous series of self instruction books that have, for the last three hundred years, successfully lined the coffers of various publishers. A few weeks after its publication the bookshelves at Waterstones were full of such titles as "The Complete Footballer", "The Complete Duck Shooter", The Complete Guide To Successful Cross-Over Buttock Throwing", and "The Complete Book of Stoat and Weasel Baiting".

It is worth considering just how influential Isaak Walton's book was. Up its publication most people looked upon the act of fishing as a necessary occupation undertaken by the lower classes in order to put food on their table. Soon after the publication of this book, throughout the length and breadth of England, the river banks were lined by the fashionable members of the upper crust dangling their rods in the vain hope that the new fangled sport would quickly die out. It didn't.

River owners soon discovered they could earn extra income by hiring out permits and licenses to fish along their stretch of river. Suddenly the poor, who couldn't afford the cost of even a day ticket, were reduced to having to use the lesser waters and smaller streams and living off smaller fish like Sticklebacks and freshwater Crayfish. However fishing the Isaak Walton way wasn't like it is today, as a quote from his book will show -

Instructions for baiting a line with a live frog.
In doing so, use him as though you loved him.

Fascinating stuff eh? If I loved my frog I'd be damn sure I didn't stick a bloody great fish hook through him, and dangle him in a river for fish to feed on, but there again, I don't go fishing, neither do I have a frog.

Overnight in many towns and villages, fishing tackle shops and live bait sellers sprang up for business. One of these was a small wooden shack near to York's North Street Postern Tower and called "Ye Olde Fyshing Tackle Shoppe for the Complete T'angler". It is not known whether the unusual name of the business was a Yorkshire dialect pun on Isaak Walton's book or whether it was simply a typographical error.

This fishing shoppe was the first of its type in the city and in its early days was treated with grave suspicion by the local residents who couldn't understand why people had to buy worms when all they had to do was turn over their own dung heap. Fishing line came as a surprise to them as up to now they had made do with lengths of strong waxed thread. They also couldn't understand the need for all those hooks when for years they had made do with a bent nail. However a careful marketing strategy undertaken by the York advertising agency run by Messers Hook, Line and Sinker soon convinced people that by using string and bent nails they hadn't caught anything in their lives, and wouldn't catch anything in the future, unless they bought the correct tackle.

In July 1662 Charles founded The Royal Society, the first ever scientific institute anywhere in Europe to enjoy royal patronage. It membership reads like a whose who from a school physics book, containing great names like Halley the astronomer and discoverer of comets, the inventor Captain Hooke, the physicist Boyle, the architect

Christopher Wren, and of course the most famous scientist of them all, Isaac Newton the discoverer of falling apples and inventor of the well known phrase "what goes up must come down!"

Towards the end of his reign Charles once again faced the age old problem of religious differences. Without having any evidence to back the claims up, some puritanical zealots had begun to claim that the Great Fire of London had been a papist plot, and as a result a nasty anti-Catholic fervour was beginning to sweep through London. Then, when a bloke called Titus Oates appeared on the scene ranting and raving claims that he had discovered a plot to murder Charles and place his Catholic brother the Duke of York on the throne, the anti-Catholic frenzy grew even wilder. Oates was eventually discredited, but only after his bogus claims had lead to more than thirty judicial murders. Despite Oates being proved a liar, just to be on the safe side, Parliament demanded that Charles excluded his brother James from any future royal succession. Talk about flinging the dirt and it sticking.

The question of succession was proving tricky enough, without disqualifying the next in line as Charles II had no children by his official marriage to Catherine of Braganza. Mind you the rumour that he fired blanks was firmly scotched by the fact that he fathered eight illegitimate children by five different mistresses. Then, just to make matters worse, Charles died in 1685 before the question could be sorted out, and so by default brother James became King James II, the first Catholic monarch on the English throne for over a hundred years.

His reign began peacefully enough but James soon fell out with Parliament when he discovered that they were seeking to enforce laws against all dissenters of the Church of England, just as he himself was attempting to secure civil equalities for all religious persuasions including Catholics, Non-conformists, Methodists, Bush Baptists and followers of the little green god called Baal.

When The Duke of Monmouth, who was Charles' favourite illegitimate son, began a Protestant revolt in the West Country, popular opinion supported James. Then the populace withdrew it again when they realised the cruelty of Judge Jefferies and his dreaded assizes that had been set up to punish the wrong doers. They also got upset when James prosecuted seven Anglian Bishops, violated the rights of the universities, and placed a number of Roman Catholics in key military positions.

Having his finger on the pulse of popular opinion, and sensing the way the wind was blowing, James quickly raised himself an army. However whatever he did, the followers of the Protestant cause were still wearing smug looks on their faces because they knew that whatever actions James took, the question of succession was settled. They knew that his successor would be a Protestant. It had finally been decided that, on the death of James, the throne would pass to his eldest daughter Mary, who had married her cousin, William, the son of Charles II's sister, thus keeping it all nicely in the family.

At the time William was the leader of the Protestant Dutch who were busy fighting the Catholic French forces of Louis XIV, and thus he seemed adequate enough to tackle the job in hand. God only knows what questions were asked at the interview. Mind you, another fact in his favour was that he was also the strongest male claimant to the throne.

William was very health conscious, and was extremely paranoid about catching colds. Indeed, in order to keep any colds at bay, as well as wearing a woolly muffler and Damart underwear, he took vitamin C in vast quantities. Indeed he took so much vitamin C that his skin turned a strange colour and in consequence, behind his back, he was nicknamed William of Haliborange.

The status quo of the succession issue was upset in 1688 when James' wife gave birth to a son. The threat of a further period of Catholic rule caused the bigots in Parliament such worry that a deputation travelled to Holland to invite William to claim the throne for himself. He landed at Brixham and marched onto London where support for James slowly melted away. Loyal subjects who were at the front of the flag waving queue when Charles arrived at Dover were suddenly very conspicuous by their absence. Sensing which way the wind was blowing once again, James quickly jumped Le Shuttle and fled to France where he lived in exile in a small Left Bank studio flat for another 12 years.

With James safely holed up in France the throne of England was technically vacant. Power was in the hands of William whilst Mary, his wife remained in Holland. To sort the matter out, and to finally decide whether he was king or not, William convened a meeting of Parliament on 1st Feb. 1689. Three weeks later everyone finally emerged, pale and blinking in the day light, to announce an agreement. This "Declaration of Rights" denounced the "illegalities" of James' reign, disbanded his army and annulled his claims to dispense law. The Declaration went even further by suggesting that William should be Regent whilst his wife Mary should be Queen. However, as the couple were utterly devoted to each other and liked to do things together, they preferred to reign jointly. Hence they were officially re-christened William'n Mary, and ruled together successfully until Mary sadly died of smallpox in 1694.

William took the death of his wife very badly and took to his bed refusing to take an interest in anything except his fight with Louis XIV. He even refused to take his vitamin C. He soon began suffering from asthma and bronchitis, and then made matters worse by taking to the drink, giving the usual excuse that it was for purely medicinal reasons.

Eventually it was explained to him that he was the King and things had to carry on. He was persuaded to get out of bed, get out and about, and start ruling things again, which was a bit of a shame as he died eight years later having suffered a serious injury falling from his horse when it tripped over a molehill in the lawns at Hampton Court.

William was succeeded by James II's daughter Anne, who, despite being only 37 years of age, was physically infirm through suffering seventeen pregnancies. Existing court records claim that she was plain, gouty, dumpy and dim. It also claimed that she was petty, argumentative and had little education or intellect. So much for the court's opinion of her. Despite that, Anne was very popular with her English subjects, mainly because she loved hunting, gambling, hated the French, and could down a pint of bitter in less than ten seconds. In short she came across as one of the lads, a thing that was guaranteed to endear her to her English subjects.

Anne must also have had great legs. They are said to have inspired many of the furniture makers of the time to invent a special, elegantly shaped table leg which they called “Queen Anne Leg”. Although whether she had ball and claw feet is very debatable

Throughout her reign Anne held a close friendship with a woman called Sarah Churchill, who took full advantage of her exalted friendship by persuading the Queen to promote her husband to the position of Duke of Marlborough. (The sycophancy of Anne’s court stretched to other of Sarah’s friends. Another good mate of hers was Sydney Godolphin who was made Lord Treasurer, and sometimes referred to as Prime Minister, the first time such a title was used.)

There is a well known saying “Come the time, come the man”, and Churchill nee Marlborough was just the chappie. Ever since William’n Mary’s reign England had been at war with the French. Now, led by Marlborough who commanded an army made up of English, Dutch, and Germans, the English managed to achieved a spectacular series of victories, the greatest of which was at Blenheim. In a battle that lasted eight hours he managed to rout the French armies killing an estimated 26,000 men and capturing another 15,000. Louis XIV could not sustain such great losses and he was forced to abandon his plans to dominate Europe. Sulking, he retired back to France and forbade anyone from ever mentioning the name of the battle in his presence again.

When the dust finally settled Marlborough was declared a great public hero and given his own palace at Blenheim to live in. He was so popular that they named streets, pubs, and popular brands of cigarettes after him. But Marlborough’s victories relied on money underpinned by popular support, especially from his influential friends at court. When Anne fell out with Sarah Churchill, the resulting fracas not only caused Marlborough a few personal problems but, as so many of Sarah’s friends had been promoted into positions of power, the row also brought down the entire Whig government. The Tories then took power and, behind everyone's backs, made peace with the French.

Anne died in 1714 after spending the last years of her life trying to sort out the age old question of succession. Parliament had banned the idea of her Catholic half brother James, who was known as the "Old Pretender" from getting anywhere near to the throne, instead demanding that the next heir should be the first available Protestant.

After a long and tedious genealogical search he turned out to be a member of The House of Hanover, Anne's German cousins. However, whilst she had been alive, Anne had detested these cousins so much that she banned any of them from ever setting foot on English soil. Eventually though, in the final years of her life, she was brought around to the idea of them succeeding her, and she hard worked to ensure that the planned succession would go ahead peacefully. An emissary was sent to Hanover to consult with the future King George I with an agreement that stated that when Anne died he was next in line for the job.

CHAPTER TWELVE

GEORGIAN YORK

The Georgian period of British history covers the reign of four monarchs, every one of them called George! This period of British history heralded an era of elegance. Throughout the country men suddenly became fashion victims. They wore huge powered wigs, tight trousers, inhaled snuff and drank coffee and port. Women quickly followed. They wore huge hairstyles piled high on their heads, and satin dresses cut so low that their bosoms were permanently on display, just like they do in the popular period television series that are done so well by the BBC.

London was now the centre of high fashion. Not to be left out, York became the social capital of the North of England. Northern gentry with their families in tow flocked to the city to see and to be seen at the summer and winter seasons. In its turn the city changed and adapted to embrace this new concept of leisure. York underwent a process called "gentrification", which in normal language means that, as it had become the fashionable place to be and to be seen in, everything in sight had to be done up, and not with just a lick of paint, it was done up as in knock it down and start all over again!

During this period many of York's older shop properties were changed into the new fangled coffee houses. The coffee house was a new concept in leisure that began during the 1670's. Originally Charles II tried to suppress them believing them to be a breeding ground for plots, counter plots, conspiracies and subterfuge, and illicit dope dealing. Mind you, in those days the same could be said of anywhere members of the general public could gather in more than two and threes. Coffee houses soon became the place where merchants, traders, business men, prominent people, and writers would meet, talk business and drink coffee, which was still a novelty and not the habit it is today.

One of the more famous writers that inhabited the coffee houses of York was Lawrence Stern author of the famous book "Tristram Pint O' Shandy".

Daniel Defoe, the creator of the fictional character of Robinson Crusoe inventor of the popular radio programme "Desert Island Discs", was also supposed to have enjoyed the odd cappuccino inside the York coffee houses. Indeed Defoe actually mentioned York in his book "Whole Island of Great Britain", written between 1722 and 1724. He wrote -

> *"York is indeed a pleasant and beautiful city........There is an abundance of good company here, and an abundance of good families live here, for the sake of the good company and the cheap living; a man converses here with all the world as effectually as at London......*
>
> *.....The ladies make a very noble appearance here, and, if I may speak my thoughts without flattery, take the like number where you will, yet, in spite of the pretended reproach of country breeding, the ladies of the north are as handsome and as well dress'd as are to be seen either at the Court or the ball."*

For him to have written that last paragraph he must have taken a walk through the Museum Gardens during a summer lunchtime when the lawns are covered by York's female office and shop workers, all trying to get a bit of a tan before going away on holiday. "Phew what a scorcher" as today's tabloids would say.

With all this coming and going it's really no surprise to find that York quickly became the main coaching centre of the north. It stood at the cross roads of two major coaching routes, the east-west coast to coast route, and the main London-Edinburgh route. The London coach left York at five a.m. on Mondays, Wednesdays and Fridays and took four uncomfortable days to complete its journey to The Black Swan in Holborn. It is said that travellers going all the way from York to London were so shaken up that, by the time they arrived at their London lodgings, they found it impossible to hold a glass of beer, a glass of wine or any other liquid , without throwing it all over themselves.

In 1706 a service between Newcastle and London via York was started. The coach left on Mondays and Fridays and the journey from York to Newcastle took two days, just a little longer than the same journey on the decrepit rolling stock currently run by the newly privatised G.N.E.R. (joke!).

Many large coaching inns sprang up in the city supplying coach travellers with food, drink, bar snacks, overnight accommodation, more drink and, in some of the more dubious establishments, a willing doxy. (It seems that the word doxy crept into the English language around this time and drifted away again soon after, destined only to reappear in Olde English folk songs. It is a quaint word that really means prostitute, or a woman of loose morals. Still its better than the more recent counterpart, the word "Slapper.")

The George and the Black Swan Inns in Coney Street, The Starre in Stonegate and The White Swan in Pavement were the coaching inns that the upper classes and well heeled chose to use. They were really the Dean Court, Holiday Inn's of their time.

The less wealthy traveller, or middle classes, used the many smaller establishments that sprang up in their wake. These places provided the middle ground for travellers comfort, equivalent to the higher range of guest house and quality private hotels you find around the city. Only in those days you could get quality stabling with hot and cold running straw in all stalls.

The Greasy Egg and Spoon, in Monkgate, The Newt and Ferret in Walmgate, The Cheese and Chutney in Marygate, and the Fiddlers Elbow in Micklegate, all represented the lower end of the market. These places specialised in serving such wondrous and nourishing food as the famous York all day breakfasts, bangers and mash, egg and chips, cow heels, tripe with or without onions, and ploughman's lunches, made with real mud, and so fresh they were stolen that very morning.

Defoe must have stayed at one of these establishments. It could only have been one of their menu's that prompted Defoe to write the following -

"Feasting to excess with one another is strongly in use in York.............

It is for this reason and their constantly living upon solid meat that few of the inhabitants arte long lived in York. The common people speak English very ill; and have a strange affected pronunciation of some words as hoose, moose, and coo for house, mouse, and cow and so on....."

Cheeky sod!

Another infamous writer that inhabited the darker regions of York's coffee houses was the performance poet Dusty Roads, better known as The Mad Poet of Tockwith. Unable to get his work published this poet would hide behind doors and panels in the coffee houses and pubs of York and suddenly leap out at the innocent drinkers and shout comedy poetry at them. Soon he was banned from all premises and was reduced to lurking around street corners and dark alleyways, shouting his work at surprised passers by. Eventually, for his own safety, he was taken into custody and locked up in York Prison. He was arrested by Constable Jimmy Fairwiggle, York's only natural blond policeman. "It's a fair cop!" Said Roads still desperately trying to get a laugh even as he was being arrested.

The rich landed gentry flocked to the city to enjoy the entertainments of the winter and spring seasons and, in order to make the place more presentable for them, yet again the city underwent a period of massive rebuilding.

All over the city ropes and red lamps began appearing. Holes were dug, filled in and dug up again. Streets such as Lord Mayor's Walk were widened and lined with elegant elm trees. Another walkway was created alongside the River Ouse at New Walk. It began where the Foss joined the Ouse, and continued along the river bank all the way to

Fulford, where a house built in 1765 by John Carr, the famous York architect, sold afternoon teas, buns, fancy cakes, and jam doughnuts. It also did a roaring trade selling under the counter jars of medicated footpowder and corn plasters.

Many of the old, half timbered, medieval buildings that had been damaged during the Civil War, (or during the celebrations that heralded the Restoration), were replaced by bright new buildings made of red brick, and a new architectural style named after the Georgian period was introduced throughout the city. The elegant Micklegate House was built in 1752 and the equally elegant Fairfax House and Castlegate House were both built in 1762. New houses were built along the main entrances to the city on The Mount, Bootham, and along Monkgate, which all became the most fashionable areas of the city, and the places where one simply had to be seen in.

Other elegant houses were built inside the city walls. In 1722 a Dr. Wintringham built his house on Lendal. When it was finished this house was so desirable that it soon became the official residence of the Judges of the Assize, the travelling judges who presided over the York Courts. Today the building houses a hotel called, surprisingly enough, "The Judges Lodgings".

Whilst it was the original "Judges Lodgings", this building was a frequent home to the infamous Judge Harold Simpson better known as "Hang'em High Harry". Being insane and senile and having an intense dislike of all forms of humanity, this Judge was deemed highly qualified to pass judgment on those more unfortunate than himself, and in some cases actual criminals. Whatever plea the plaintiff may have made in their defence, Judge Simpson always took the same approach, "Hang em!". In short, he showed the exact judicial qualities that one would expect from a man whose hobbies were listed in "Who's Who" as fox hunting, fly fishing, grouse shooting, hare coursing, badger baiting, weasel whipping, stoat stamping, and vole strangling. For him the qualities of mercy were not strained and did not drop from heaven onto the earth below, but were better served by a body swinging from a rope on a gibbet.

When Simpson was in his late eighties he eventually went too far and was removed from the bench after the famous incident at York Assize in 1732 when, not only did he order the prisoner to be hung for stealing a loaf of bread, he also ordered the defence barrister to be hanged for having bushy eyebrows, the clerk of the court to be hanged for writing with a squeaky quill, and the entire jury to be hanged because they hadn't washed behind their necks and had dirty finger nails. When he was told his judgment was misguided and that he was a certifiable loony he lost it completely and was lead away from the court frothing at the mouth and screaming obscenities at the greatly amused onlookers..

As anyone born North of Leeds and South of Newcastle knows, anything London can do York can do better. York's Mansion House, the official home of the Lord Mayor was built in 1730, several years before London eventually got around to building one for itself. York is so proud of this fact that it is repeated in just about every history book ever written about the city. Or at least, in those written after 1730!

Throughout the latter half of the century, throughout the city, major building operations continued unabated. Roads were opened and closed with regularity. The ropes and red lamps put around the many holes in the road had become permanent features and everyone grumbled and wondered if the city would ever get finished.

Micklegate Bar was altered by John Carr who made two extra arches on either side of the main entrance to enable the increased traffic flow to get in and out of the City. New Street was opened in 1746 when Davy Hall was demolished enabling the link between Davygate and Coney Street to be developed. In 1769 both Spurriergate and Pavement, were widened, and widened once again in the following century. Goodramgate was widened in 1771, as was Skeldergate in an operation that involved the moving and rebuilding of Anne Middleton's Hospital. St. Helen's Square, previously the graveyard of St. Helen's Church, was created and opened up in 1780. Duncombe Place, a Georgian modernisation of the medieval Lop Lane, was opened in 1785, and Museum Street was opened in 1791. Castlegate Postern Lane was transformed into Castlegate in 1806.

Street lighting first illuminated the streets of York in 1724 and it was such a success that it was extended in 1763. For the first time in their history, during the periods of darkness, York's citizens could actually see what they were treading in. Now they actually knew what it was that made the strange "gloop" noise as they trod on it, and they didn't like it! The many deputations made to the City Council forced them to instigate a policy of street sweeping and cleaning, an idea that was extended throughout the all the city streets in 1786. Even then the true gentry didn't really like risking their expensive footwear by treading on the streets and so they employed servants to carry them around in Sedan chairs.

Eventually many of the city's unpaved streets were cobbled and stoned, (a feeling familiar to many York people theses days!). The Corporation even employed a paver who looked after the pavements in front of their own properties, whilst every private householder in the city was made responsible for the paving and its upkeep in front of their own properties, as well as for keeping their bit of the street clean.

An Act of Parliament, passed in 1763, also made householders responsible for providing drainpipes to channel water from their house roofs. It seems that, prior to 1763, one of the most objectionable aspects of urban living was that, when it rained, anyone walking along a pavement would suddenly get drenched by water pouring off the roofs of houses. A wetting guaranteed to ruin their powdered wigs, and which made them appear as if they were all carrying drowned cats on their heads.

Personally I think that anyone walking through the streets in the pouring rain should expect something like that to happen, but there again, I've been brought up in a society that benefited from the invention of the umbrella and where the common drainpipe has been taken for granted for generations. Perhaps the sight of some wig wearing, painted Georgian fop getting a sudden drenching wasn't as funny then as it seems now!

Another major civic improvement was the introduction of piped water. York Waterworks was founded in 1682 in St. Leonard's Tower where a horse drawn engine was installed to pump water from the Ouse to all parts of the town via a series of wooden pipes. However this wasn't hot and cold running water as we know it today, it was just cold and it didn't run very well either. The pipes leaked and, as the company could never meet supply with demand, water was only available on tap on certain days of the week.

The establishment of the County Hospital, and the Bootham Park Asylum made York into something of a medical center. Doctors and patients flocked to the town and a new mini industry of "healthy" cures began to establish itself. However around this period the nearby town of Harrogate began to promote their evil smelling sulfur springs as a cure-all and the invalid tourist trade immediately flocked there instead.

Schools were established, as were Almshouses and a number of Nonconformist churches. After the Restoration, throughout the country, there was a period of religious toleration. In York new religions and their places of worship sprang up all over the place. The Utilitarians built their imposing chapel on St. Saviourgate and The Society of Friends, better known as the Quakers, created a meeting house in Friargate. Soon other religious persuasions built their churches and chapels in the city. Catholics, Baptists, Methodists, Weslyan Methodists, Primitive Methodists, United Methodists, Disunited Methodists, Methodical Methodists, Presbyterians, Moravians, Sandmanians, Sun Worshipers, and even followers of the tiny green god Baal all established premises in the city.

However not all changes and urban improvements are for the better and today's learned historians and architects still criticise the city council for the destruction of what they considered once fine buildings. Market Square, a small square building standing on columns was demolished in 1813, and two years later the building known as the Thursday Market Cross was demolished. Still as every member of a City Council knows, you can make an omelette without breaking eggs, and you can't please all of the people all of the time. Mainly because not everyone likes omelettes.

York was a still major market town. It had a corn market, a wool market in St. Anthony's Hall, a hay market in King's Square, a butter market in Micklegate, and down by the riverside docks were establishments that sold coal, salt, lime and the small little things that only sailors want to know about! Throughout the 18th century a number of newer industries sprang up that included comb making, horn making, drug manufacture, toys, a glassworks, flour mills and of course banks. Three opened up in 1771. As well as these new enterprises, two more small shops opened their doors for the first time.

The first was a small grocers shop opened in 1725 in Castlegate. The owner was a thirty year old woman called Mary Tuke. Despite a seven year struggle with the Merchant Adventurers Company she expanded into tea selling. This business was taken over in 1752 by her nephew William Tuke. In 1785, his son joined the company and together they began to manufacture coca and chocolate, more of which later.

The second shop was opened in St. Helen's Square by Bayldon and Berry in 1767 was also destined to become famous when it became Terry's and the population of York could now look forward to getting chocolate oranges in their Christmas stockings.

As well as being a major market town, York was also a center for crafts, and entertainment. Twice a year the city held the Assizes and it also held the York horse races. The finest day's entertainment for members of the Georgian gentry would be to flock in large numbers to the Knavesmire to watch a public hanging or two and then pop down to Clifton Ings and lose a packet on slow horses and faster women. However, Clifton Ings was subject to flooding, which made for very heavy ground and where only horses with webbed feet and fitted with water wings stood a chance of winning. In 1730 a new race course was founded on the Knavesmire, which made it much handier for the people who had just witnessed the hangings, and where, in 1754, John Carr the famous York Architect was commissioned to build a new Grandstand.

The success of this grandstand brought John Carr other commissions in the city. Throughout the years York Castle had slid into disrepair. The south gate had been given up as a bad job and walled up in 1708. In 1734 the existing entrance in Castlegate was rebuilt. A new prison, originally called The County Prison had been built inside the wall facing Clifford's Tower. Then the judges of the assizes, spoilt by staying at The Judges Lodgings, wanted a better work environment and commissioned themselves a new court house, and Carr got the job. When it was finished in 1777 the judges were so pleased with it that they carried out their duties with increased vigor. Soon more prison space was needed and Carr got the job of building another prison block opposite the court. This new building, completed in 1780, became known as the Woman's Prison.

As more and more visitors flocked into the city they needed more and more entertainments or assemblies as they preferred to call them. These assemblies comprised parties, dances, card games and general gatherings where everyone paraded in the latest fashions whilst others held whispered conversations about them behind their backs. At first these assemblies were held in King's Manor, but then moved to Sir Arthur Ingrams new house by the Minster. The idea of building a special Assembly Rooms was promoted in a public broadsheet published in 1730. Everyone seemed keen enough on the idea and the project was completed just in time for the races of 1732.

The architect was Richard Boyle, better known as Lord Burlington the builder of famous shopping arcades. He designed the building, which stands on Blake Street, in a style known as Roman Corinthian, and heavily influenced by the works of a 16th century Italian architect called Palladio, from which the London Palladium is named after. Soon Blake Street became the focus of dances, parties, and other wild gatherings which in those days were known as routs.

Personally I think it's a pity that the word rout has fallen out of use today as the phrase "Do you fancy going out for a good rout?" sounds a lot more inviting than saying "Do you fancy popping down t' pub for a pint?"

In addition to the Assembly Rooms many other new leisure based buildings sprang up. In 1736 a theatre was built, there was a cock fighting pit in Bootham, a bowling green off Micklegate and even a licensed brothel in Petergate, which was pretty liberal minded for a corporation that, in 1742, banned nude bathing beside New Walk.

Mind you, there were even more perverse entertainments for the blood thirsty Georgian thrill seekers. In addition to attractions offered by the public hangings on the Knavesmire, from the years between 1745 and 1754 visitors could walk down to Micklegate Bar to view the severed heads of the failed Jacobite Rebels, and no doubt, buy suitable souvenirs, such as T-shirt's, tea towels, pottery thimbles and postcards.

During the early Georgian period a house in the Peasholme Green area of the city was owned by a famous York character known as Weevil the Vole Strangler, whose name was synonymous with his job. In 1733 York was plagued by an infestation of voles. It is believed that they bred unknown in the full sewers and river banks of the Ouse, until one day they were disturbed by rising water and burst over the unsuspecting city carrying a wave of disease and panic.

Weevil, who was normally a quiet man and whose idea of the high life was a plate of pigs trotters with his pint, became a local hero when, in an attempt to stop a wave of voles getting to his food, he single handedly strangled over four hundred of the small furry mammals. As a reward he was made a Freeman of the City and the grateful citizens gave him a small pension which enabled him to live out his life in luxury with free pints and free pigs trotters for the rest of his days. For many years the man was a familiar figure around York and, as old man, he spent most of his days dressed in a special suit of clothing made up of voleskin, sitting in the museum gardens trying to look up the skirts of any young office girls that walked by.

Meanwhile York's other river, the Foss began to gain importance. Up to the 17th century it had flowed into the large man made lake known as the King's Fish Pool and it's only use had been as a large, effective and very smelly open sewer. By the beginning of the 1700's the King's Fish Pool had decreased in size and two islands had formed near to Layerthorpe Bridge.

In 1793 it was finally decided that, as no King had ever turned up to fish in his pool for at least three hundred years, the crown probably wouldn't miss it and so attempts were made to drain it. That same year a company called The Foss Navigation Company was formed with the intent of making the Foss navigable as far as Stillington. Great excitement and expectations were created with the building of the Castle Mills lock, and when a bend in the river was made into a wharf , known as Wormalds Cut it looked as if York was in for an efficient new transport route. By 1795 the canal reached Strensall, and two years later it got as far as Sheriff Hutton. Unfortunately it was to go no further. Interest waned, money and funding dried up, work stopped and York managed to miss out on the industrial boom that other towns who had actually completed their canals, were now enjoying.

By the end of the century York had regained its vitality and was as important as it had been at its height during the medieval period. It now stretched well beyond the old city walls and began to devour up the smaller surrounding villages such as Acomb, Fulford and Clifton which soon became residential suburbs of the city.

Before we leave the Georgian period it's worth noting that this period also saw a couple of the more colourful characters that inherited the title of Duke Of York. Edward Augustus, Duke of York from 1739-67, was the younger brother of King George III. Despite being described as "remarkably plain with strange loose eyes" the bloke must have had something about him because he became famous for the number of mistresses he had. In order to prevent scandals breaking out his royal relations packed him off into the Navy. He was given the Freedom of the City in 1761, a couple of years before dying from a fever he caught when, after attending a particularly sweaty all night ball, he galloped through the pouring rain to meet one of his many mistresses.

The 11th Duke of York was called Frederick, and was the second son of George III. He was the Grand Old Duke Of York, made famous by the nursery rhyme that accused him of marching his army of ten thousand men up a hill and marching them back down again.

This doggerel actually refers to his unsuccessful exploits whilst he was Commander-In-Chief of the army under Wellington and was away fighting the French in Holland. The joke being that there are no hills in Holland, once again, not exactly the wit of modern stand-up comedy, but it probably had them rolling in the aisles back then.

Mind you, the guys career was also littered by scandals involving his mistresses. As with most tabloid stories, it completely ignores the fact that the man was popular with his troops and highly praised by Wellington for his administrative capabilities. Still once the mud is thrown it tends to stick. As many of today's politicians and public figures know to their own cost, if you're caught in the wrong bed, with the wrong person, at the wrong time, someone somewhere will find out and publish the story, and its doesn't matter a twopenny damn how good you are at your job.

Whatever these blokes did I think they have to be a damn sight more interesting and colourful than the present day Duke and Duchess of York. I mean, who do we have today? A helicopter pilot and the creator of the children's book "Budgie the Helicopter"!

CHAPTER THIRTEEN

NINETEENTH CENTURY YORK

At the start of the nineteenth century York was once again a city in decline. The Industrial Revolution had begun around 1759, and by 6 o'clock everyone had stopped for tea. As there were no new industries in the town its dawning made very little impact on York itself, but it did gave birth to the financial success, and phenomenal growth of the industrial towns of the West Riding.

York was no longer the Northern capital it had been in Georgian times. The fickle finger of fashion had pointed to pastures and pleasures new and the gentry were no longer fascinated by public hangings, horse racing, cock fighting and coffee houses, they had found new diversions and new places to do them in.

Indeed in 1802 the public executions were moved from the Knavesmire into the precinct of York Castle, onto St. George's Field, where in 1813 thousands gathered to see the public execution of seventeen men in one day. These unfortunates were Luddites, the smashers and wreckers of new machinery that threatened their jobs and livelihoods. Which, when you think about it, is a natural reaction to anything that threatens ones wage and home. I remember the Wapping riots of 1986 when Rupert Murdoch moved his printing presses from central London to Docklands, on the way picking up new technology and ditching around 5,000 print workers. You can't stop progress, but I'm damn certain that the workforce whose jobs have just been taken over by a microchip should be offered a better option than the dole.

However the new industries of the 1800's shunned York due to a number of different factors. The high price of coal, the stranglehold on trade that was held by the Guilds, and the fact that only Freemen could trade in the city. Despite the markets still flourishing, York's economy soon became stagnant. It's interesting to note that around this period of time the largest group of workers in York were domestic servants, builders and leather workers. That must tell us something about York society in this period, although what it actually tells us I'm not too sure. Unemployment was high and the poor had to depend on private charities, begging, mugging and thieving to earn their crusts.

One of the more colourful criminals from this period was a bloke called Spring Bottomed Bobby. This enterprising burglar attempted to emulate the crimes of the notorious Spring Heeled Jack, only Bobby took the concept one stage further. Bobby invented a horse drawn carriage that had a large spring hidden under the drivers seat. He would drive the carriage under the windows of a house he wanted to burgle and pull a catch, releasing the spring. Then he would be propelled high into the air, grab hold of a passing window sill and gain entry into the upper floors of the house.

At least that was the theory, on many occasions his exploits went horribly wrong. The spring would become too taut and Bobby could often be seen flying through the night air, high over the city rooftops, screaming like a deranged Mary Poppins. He was eventually arrested whilst hanging by his braces from the guttering of the newly built Yorkshire Bank Building in St. Helen's Square. He was tried, found guilty and transported to Australia, where, as well as undergoing a sex change operation, was also inspired by the native kangaroo. He/she then attached springs to his/her feet and was last seen bouncing off into the outback where he/she founded the township of Alice Springs. Meanwhile, back in York, Bobby's ideas were pinched by a bloke called Hansom who ripped out the spring and converted the carriage into a horse drawn taxi, which he called, surprisingly enough, a Hansom Cab.

Despite the many hardships one York firm was doing very nicely thank you. The metal working company of Walkers, founded in 1800, were busy making ornate iron gates and railings. They got the commission to make the railings and gates for Queen Victoria's Palace at Sandringham, the railings that surround The British Museum, and a number of York shop fronts and railings. An example of their work can be seen in the entrance gates to the Dean's Park gates, leading up to the Minster Library. Another fine example of their work can still be seen an the Royal Botanical Gardens......in Mauritius. One reason for their popularity was their innovative after sales policy of giving a free crowbar and a jar of goose grease to every purchaser so they could prise the heads of small boys out of the newly installed railings without bothering the fire brigade.

New housing continued to be built in the ever expanding York suburbs, and new building developments continued inside the city walls. The Mount was developed further. The cattle market was moved from Walmgate to a new site outside the walls, where the Barbican building now stands. The market in Pavement was now selling corn, poultry, eggs, butter and fruit and desperately needed more space. A number of old buildings were demolished to make a way through to the site of the old Thursday market. This opening formed the new Parliament Street and became home for the new larger and improved market place that ran down the centre of the new street.

A huge forty foot wide swathe was cut through the area north of the unused St. Leonard's Hospice and a terrace of elegant Georgian style houses were built. These houses were later converted and are now council offices. However the building of St. Leonard's created a dangerous precedent. It cut through and destroyed some of the medieval city walls.

The City Corporation then took one step further towards loonyville when they actually promoted the idea of destroying all the city walls and bars. Fortunately, just in time, it was discovered that they didn't have the legal right to do such a thing, bit it still didn't stop them from having a jolly good go. In 1808 they removed Skeldergate Postern, and in 1810 suggested tearing down Micklegate Bar. There was a public outcry led by a York artist called William Etty, and, wanting to save their jobs and necks, the Corporation eventually bowed to pubic opinion. Instead they undertook a policy of sneak removal. This meant that, in the middle of the night, when no one was looking, they ran out and knocked bits down. In 1825 they came up with the idea of demolishing Clifford's Tower, but had second thoughts and contented themselves with destroying the barbican of Monk Bar in 1825, that of Micklegate Bar in 1826, the same year that Layerthorpe Postern mysteriously disappeared one night. The following year they destroyed

Castlegate Postern. In 1831 they suggested knocking down Bootham Bar but again, after more public uproar, they satisfied themselves with just knocking down its barbican.

After a yet another public meeting, the York Footpath Association was formed with the intent of creating a public walkway around the York walls, and over the next few years they succeeded in their vision. It is safe to say that this walkway idea saved the Walls of York, but still the Corporation were not satisfied. Despite restoring Walmgate's Barbican in 1840, they decided to knock it down again in 1855. Once again they had to give way to public opinion, did an about turn, and restored once again it in 1864.

But those were the losses, William Etty's major victory was saving the majority of the walls and bars from the Corporation whom, he christened as "Vandals". It is worth pondering what York would look like today if William Etty had not led the first protest. The city would be just another northern town and would have no walls, no bars, no visitors, no tourism, no jobs, and be a very sorry place indeed. Today everyone in the City who has anything to do with tourism should, on the anniversary of his birth, go down on their bended knees and give praise and thanks for William Etty, and the fact that, without knowing it, he saved an industry that wasn't even thought off yet, one that would not surface for another century. If the employees of York Councils Tourism Department and those of Guide Friday would like to know where they should go to give thanks, the grave of William Etty can be found in the graveyard of St. Olav's Church, Marygate. Failing that, on Remembrance Day they should place a wreath on the base of his statue that stands outside the York Art Gallery. As a footnote it's worth mentioning that some of his paintings can be found inside the building, and are well worth looking at.

Meanwhile other "improvements" to the city were created. The Yorkshire Philosophical Society was founded in 1823 to "promote the diffusion of scientific knowledge generally and more particularly the elucidation of the geology, natural history and antiquities of Yorkshire". In an attempt to popularise their knowledge they deemed that the residents of York would benefit from a museum and so they employed the architect William Wilkins, designer of the National Gallery, to construct their museum building in the grounds of St. Mary's Abbey.

The establishment of this museum came just in time for the boom in scientific interest that was spawned by the publication of Darwin's "Origin of Species", in 1859 and the subsequent furor caused by various outraged traditionalists who refused to believe that is was possible that they descended from monkeys, preferring instead to believe in the biblical version of events.

York, of course, had it's own scientist who dared to challenge established belief. Dr. Arthur Pettigrew lived in the Coney Street area and, until Darwin published his theory, was a pleasant enough sort of bloke who spent his time growing ferns. However after reading the work Dr. Pettigrew suddenly and for reasons best known to himself, decided that mankind had descended from a small fern like spore that had been attached to a giant meteorite from the surface of the planet Zog that had crashed to earth at the end of the last Ice Age. When it was pointed out to him that there actually wasn't a planet Zog he claimed that "it was out there somewhere and that when it was discovered giant ferns would take over the earth!" If he hadn't belonged to certain "gentleman's clubs" and trade associations he would have been carted away. As it was he was given a strict telling off and told not be so bloody stupid. He later changed his profession to selling house plants, and making guest appearances in The X Files.

A blind school was established in King's Manor in 1833, the same year as the establishment of The Minster Song School. The Minster also established a new Residence for the Canons Residentiary in 1825 and new Deanery building in 1827. They were both completed and everyone moved in just in time to sit in their gardens and watch York Minster burn down, twice!

The first fire was caused by a man who is today politely referred to as a religious manic. Bloody nutter would be a better way of describing Jonathan Martin! He was convinced that God had spoken to him personally and, over a long and protracted series of conversations, told him to burn down York Minster. So one night after evensong,

Martin hid behind a handy tomb. When the building was deserted he crept out and built a huge mountain of hymn books, which he promptly set fire to. Leaving them to blaze away he let himself out of the building by climbing up the scaffolding and dropping out of a window.

The following morning a group of choir boys were amusing themselves by sliding on ice whilst waiting for the morning service to begin. One of them fell over and, lying flat on his back, suddenly noticed a huge plume of smoke billowing out of the Central Tower. The alarm was raised but not before the East End of the building had turned into a blazing inferno. The fire destroyed all but two of the original choir stalls and severely damaged the building. Martin was eventually caught, declared mad and spent the rest of his days dribbling in a lunatic asylum. No care in the community in those days!

In commemoration of this event the souvenir makers of York produced a cheerful little medal that gave the dates of the two previous fires, the date 1829 and three images of Martin himself. One as a normal person, labelled "What I was". One of him chained to some sort of chair labelled "What I am", and a third showing him hanging from a gibbet labelled "What I should be!". So much for the Victorian understanding of mental illness.

Eleven years later the Minster caught fire once again. This time the central vault of the nave was destroyed when a careless worker accidentally left a candle burning one night. The history books don't mention him by name and he's successfully managed to slip away from the slings and arrows of outrageous memories. However I'd put a large amount of money on the fact that he was the ancestor of the bloke that turned up to fix my central heating last winter and who managed to set fire to the cat with his blowlamp.

For some years previously, ever since James Watt had scalded himself on a kettle, various other people had been experimenting with steam powered engines, using them in the wide variety in industries that sprang up all over Britain. Steam engines were seen in mines, woollen mills and textile factories. However in 1816 the citizens of York were scared out of their wits when a noisy boat came chugging up the Ouse from Selby billowing great clouds of smoke and steam behind it.

When they eventually plucked up enough courage and ventured down the King's Staith to have a look at what was going on, instead of finding the water born, fire breathing dragon, they expected they saw the "Waterloo Steam Packet", the first ever steam ship to arrive in the city.

A few years later, in 1825, the first railway engine chugged out of Stockton to make its historic trip all the way to nearby Darlington, and a full stop was finally added to the age of Georgian Elegance. It was now replaced by the more austere Victorian Age of the Black and Smoky Steam Engine.

After taking a cheap day return trip to see the new railway, and taking a peep into the workshops, Whistling Jimmy Ramsbottom, the owner of Ye Olde Yorke Coffee House, Bakery and Writers Workshop, situated at the corner of Jubbergate and Parliament Street, realised for himself the wonders of steam power. He invested heavily into railways and steam driven expresso coffee machines.

Fascinated by engines he took them to pieces and reassembled them until he figured out how they worked. In a short space of time he became a leading inventor, working at the cutting edge of creating steam machinery for the catering industry. Unfortunately one day he caught himself on the cutting edge and could never put a hole in a doughnut again. However this painful accident gave him the inspiration for one of his greatest inventions, "The Ramsbottom Hole Maker and Jam Putter In-er", better known in the industry as a "Steaming Ram Jam". This machine was very similar in construction to a steam engine, only instead of driving wheels the steam piston drove a bloody great metal spike up and down. A secondary piston pumped hot raspberry jam into a concealed cylinder set inside the spike and, as the spike reached the end of its forward thrust, hot jam squirted out of its tip. So powerful was this machine that it is said that the effect of seeing it go through its motions could scare a timid person off sex for the rest of their lives.

Another great Ramsbottom invention was the steam driven batter mixer, capable of mixing enough batter to supply over three thousand fish and chip shops at the same time. Unfortunately, as it was the size of a small detached house, it was too big and he sold the idea to a mate of his called Ken Wood, who waited until the invention of electricity and then miniaturised it.

However Jimmy's reputation in the catering industry suffered a terrible blow when he invented the Ramsbottom Plunger. Due to a misprint in his press release, Tiny Mullett the editor of a local York newspaper, reviewed this new invention thinking it was a sex toy. The starchy, upright Victorian community of York immediately ostracised Jimmy, using his own ostriches. As the scandal broke he was hauled up in front of a special committee of MP's and given a secret research job working for the governments whips office. Sadly he was never heard of again.

When Whistling Jimmy Ramsbottom left York the Corporation of the town brought the lease of his property and changed the premises to become a much needed Police Holding Cell. It appears that York was in the middle of a crime wave and the jails were all full of miscreants and general no gooders. More overnight accommodation was urgently needed where criminals, caught in the middle of the city, could be quickly locked up whilst the police filled in the necessary paperwork before transferring them to the more prestigious accommodation offered by York's Castle Prison. The inside of these cells have held some desperate criminals, and been witness to many dark deeds.

A York fishmonger was in fact the notorious fish strangler known as Jack the Kipper. He was single handedly responsible for the deaths of over two thousand small chubb in the River Foss. In the middle of the night, dressed only in a pair of large rubber waders and an old raincoat, he would stand waist deep in the river with his hands outstretched into the water. Then as a fish would swim by he would quickly move his hands and flip it onto the nearby bank where it would thrash around. Armed with a deadly gutting knife "The Kipper" would surgically remove its entrails, which he would then festoon on the railings outside the Mansion House. He would then smoke the rest of the fish over an open fire and sell them to unsuspecting shoppers at York Market.

These perverse decorations on the railings upset everyone who saw them, especially the Lord Mayor who not only lived in the Mansion House but was allergic to fish. Eventually Jack was caught, tried and imprisoned. It is said that on a special night when the moon is in a certain quarter you can still get a faint sniff of smoked fish and old waders from the cell he was thrown into.

Dick O'Turpentine has been described as one of England's most evil poisoners and his attempts at poisoning the entire city of York are now legendary. Dick was a humble market trader specialising in the selling of cut price paperware until one day a bad attack of Montezuma's revenge hit the Shambles area. It is said that "it's an ill wind blows somebody some good", and throughout the Shambles there was certainly a very ill wind. Within a day Dick sold out of his entire stock of loo rolls. Thinking that the attack would run through the city Dick bought up all the stocks of loo paper he could lay his hands on. However the infection never spread outside of the small area and within a couple of days it had all blown over and Dick was left holding a huge warehouse size stock of loo paper.

It was then that he had his despicable idea. His mate, an unsavory character named "One Eyed Tom", had a pie and peas shop at the corner of St. Samson's Square and, with the prospect of a few free pints and a cut of the proceeds, Tom was persuaded to aid and abet the crime. It would soon be the feast day of St. Celia of the Holy Pea Pod when the citizens of York would venture out into the streets to get drunk and eat pie and peas. Dick's plan was to lace the mushy peas with turpentine, and it was a spectacular success. The day after the religious feast day there was a long queue of anxious, cross legged York citizens outside his shop all demanding loo paper. Indeed such was the effect of eating this mixture that many of the citizens were so stricken that they thought the world was falling out of their bottom. They dare not leave their houses for days and Dick had to begin a door to door delivery service, for which he charged a premium fee.

It was only after the city returned to normal that people began to put two and two together. Dick O'Turpintine was arrested and most of the affected citizens said he should be bloody well hung. When the police threw him into the cell they removed his trousers and discovered that he was.

Blind Pew the Silly Mugger was probably the most unsuccessful mugger the history of crime has ever seen. Unable to see his victims approaching, Blind Pew would hide behind doors, street corners and alleyways listening for, and sniffing out, any approaching people. Unfortunately his sensory deprivation never told him how big the approaching people were. Many were the occasions when Blind Pew would jump out of the shadows only to have seven shades of shit beaten out of him by some rugby playing, prop row forward on his way home from a busy night of anvil throwing.

Pew was finally arrested in the gents toilet of a York hostelry, standing in front of a new fangled "speak your weight" machine holding a gun to its dial and demanding it give him all its money. Eventually, along with other felons, cut throats, highwaymen and general ne'r do wells, Blind Pew was thrown into the new York prison which had been completed in 1825.

In building this new prison, rows of houses in Castlegate, and North Gate had been demolished, making way for the building of a great gray wall of solid millstone grit thirty five feet high. This imposing and intimidating wall completely enclosed the existing prison buildings, the court buildings as well as Clifford's Tower. It would be over hundred years before York residents would ever see it again.

Towards the end of the century, the number of military establishments in York began to increase. The Calvary Barracks had originally been built between Fulford Road and Walmgate Stray at the end of the eighteenth century. In 1874 the Infantry Barracks was built next door, and two years later Strensall Common was taken over for use as both barracks and firing ranges. Around the same period York Prison ceased to be a civil prison and was used solely as a military detention center.

One of the reasons for all this military activity was that Britain hadn't fought a decent war since winning away from home against Napoleon, 40 years earlier, and the powers that be thought it was time to flex some muscle. Not only that but the factory owners and manufacturing barons all felt that a good war would stimulate the economy, and fill their order books. Everyone felt pretty confident when the government, suspecting that Russia's recent declaration of war on Turkey was just a flimsy excuse for the Russians to get nearer British India, allied itself to Turkey. Just for good measure France joined in as well. A fortnight later on May 31st 1854, Britain declared war on Russia and an expeditionary force was sent out to The Black Sea

The subsequent Crimean War, famous for the invention of such things as failed charges, light brigades, sandwiches, balaclavas, nightingales, and cardigans, was to last for two years before Russia, seeing that Austria was getting ready to join in, quickly signed a peace treaty and the British troops came back home again.

However they'd no sooner unpacked their old kit bags and warmed their feet in their own barracks before they were all shipped off to India to sort out a Mutiny and then get themselves involved in a bit of bother in China. Wisely enough the powers that be chose to stay neutral for the American Civil War, deciding that as it was only a civil matter it would be impolite, not to mention uncivil, to join in without being invited. Besides that they had troubles of their own. British troops were fighting in Afghanistan and getting themselves ready for the outbreak of the Boer War in 1880, which carried on more or less to the end of the century,

Meanwhile back in York, the horses that drove the engines of York's waterworks were replaced by a large steam engine that raised 18 gallons a stroke and pumped 18 strokes a minute. This steam engine also created hot water and, following the old adage that says an opportunist is someone, who finding themselves in hot water, decides to take a bath, York Waterworks opened the towns first steam baths. A hot night bath cost 3/6, a hot day bath 2/-, whilst tepid and cold baths could be had for 6d. Of course for the many poor people the river was still the only free option, that and dancing naked in the rain. However any citizens who tried the later preference soon found themselves locked up in the Bootham Park lunatic asylum.

In 1846 a new water works, complete with filter beds was built at Acomb Landing, and domestic baths began to be built inside some of the larger more grand houses. By the turn of the century around ten percent of York houses contained baths.

Always keeping abreast of the latest fashion trends, and recognising a good thing when they saw it, the people of York were soon wanting a railway for themselves, and in 1840 the first railway line, built by the York and North Midland Company, reached the city from Normanton, 15 miles away, where it joined with the Leeds & Selby Railway.

The following year, when Normanton was connected to North Midland Railway, York has its first direct rail connection with London. It took fourteen hours to reach the capital, a time which was cut in 1848 when the Great Northern Railway created another route into York, the one still used today, when the journey time has been cut to two and a half hours, unless there are leaves on the line and drivers to operate the trains!

Other railway lines came into York. The city was soon connected with Darlington and Newcastle by the Great North of England Railway Company. The York and North Midland Company constructed the Scarborough line in 1845, and in 1846 a line to Market Weighton and onto Beverley was constructed. In 1848 The East and West Yorkshire Company opened a line to Knaresborough.

Most of these small railway companies amalgamated and merged, becoming part of the North Eastern Railway Company which in turn, in 1923, became the London and North Eastern Company, the famous L.N.E.R.

All these railway lines needed somewhere for them to end, where passengers could get on and off, and a railway station was built at Tanner Row in 1841. It was designed by an architect called G T

Andrews who was also responsible for the design of the Yorkshire Bank Building on the corner of St. Helen's Square. At the end of the railway lines a new hotel was built in which Queen Victoria, Prince Albert and five royal children stopped off at for lunch in 1853 on their way to Scotland. Mind you, it seems she didn't reckon much to the place as she never stopped in York again!

As this Tanner Row site was inside the city walls three new entrances had to made in them, however despite the expense, it was soon very apparent that this station had been built in the wrong place. It was all right as a terminus, indeed as a terminus it was ideal. The only problem was that people wanted to go further north than York. Tanner Row was impossible as a through line, mainly due to the fact that if the line was to continue, it would have to cross the Ouse and straight thorough the city center, which obviously wasn't a very good idea, despite what some members of the council thought.

Eventually another site, just outside the city walls, was chosen and a second station was built. Designed by Thomas Prosser, and completed in 1877, this new station was described as "a very splendid monument of extravagance". It's triple arched roof covered eight railway lines and its main platform stretched for 500 yards, at the time the longest in Britain.

Of course the story of York's railways cannot be complete without a mention of George Hudson, the city's Victorian equivalent of Robert Maxwell, only George didn't go swimming. Hudson was entirely responsible for York's railway industry, which may not be much now, but was a major employer from the 1840's until the twin whammies of Dr. Beeching and the last Tory government.

Hudson was the son of a wealthy farmer, lived in Monkgate and owned a draper's shop near to St. William's college. His rise to infamy began in the 1830's when he realised railways would be the next "big thing" and began buying shares. They proved to be a much better investment than a lottery ticket. Overnight he became very rich. Then, not content with being just a shareholder, Hudson began to build his own railway companies, starting with one that connected York to Leeds and then London. He was the bloke that said to George Stevenson "Make all t'railways cum t'York" and so they did, but only the railway companies owned by him! In the 1840's, at the height of his power, his empire controlled 1,500 miles of line that stretched from York to London, Bristol, Norwich and Berwick.

Hudson's influence was soon felt throughout York. He controlled the local paper, "The Yorkshire Gazette". He was director of York Union Banking Company, and The York Union Gas Lighting Company. He entered politics and became the leader of the York Tories. Three times he was made Lord Mayor and even became a Member of Parliament. The York Corporation even named a street after him. Surprisingly enough, and showing very little imagination, they called it "George Hudson Street". In short George was rich, powerful and influential, the archetypal successful entrepreneur. Everyone, especially those whom were in his employ and those for whom he made money, thought the sun shone out of his bottom. He could do no wrong, as he walked through the city streets babies were held up for him to kiss. The ill and lame would ask him to bless them and the city's bank managers thought he could walk on water. In recognition of his power he was nicknamed "The Railway King".

Mind you, you don't get that big without making enemies. Under Hudson's leadership the Tories held the majority of seats in the Corporation. He also ensured that only Tory MP's ever represented the constituency of York, much to the chagrin of George Leeman, the leader of the Liberal Whig party, and chairman of a rival railway company. It's pretty fair to say that the two of them didn't see eye to eye.

Using his influence Hudson persuaded many people to invest in his companies and, throughout the early 1840's shares in railways rose spectacularly. Investors who played the stock market made great killings and large fortunes. But, in 1848, there was a slump and hundreds of investors lost their money and were ruined. As always in these cases everyone looked for a scapegoat and there, on top of the pile was George. In 1849 his affairs were investigated and eventually he was accused of cooking the books!

His downfall was a national event and he was dismissed from all his public offices. In York his name was associated with something that dropped out of cows bottoms and he was forced to resign the chairmanship of his many companies. The council even renamed George Hudson Street, giving it the equally imaginative name of "Railway Street", and his portrait was taken down from the walls of the mansion house. In short everyone tried their best to make sure he would soon be forgotten.

Eventually he fled the country to Calais where he died penniless in 1871. What a bloke! Definitely worth lifting a couple of pints to his memory so it's sad that the only pub commemorating him once called "The Railway King" now calls itself Edward's. Mind you on the centenary of his birth, in 1971, the council relented and renamed "Railway Street". They called it George Hudson Street once again! Incidentally after Hudson fall from grace Leeman turned the political tables and became M.P. as well as being three times Lord Mayor of York. There is a even a pub named after him, The George Leeman, oddly enough on a street named Leeman Road.

Mind you the arrival of the railway wasn't good news for the many York people employed in the coaching industry. In 1830 York was still one of the main coaching centres in England when 36,000 passengers travelled to Leeds, 76,000 to Selby, and 23,000 to London, and that didn't take into account goods wagons. The city employed large numbers of coachmen, ostlers, stable boys, postmen, inn keepers, serving men, bar maids, waitresses, chamber maids and blokes that followed the horses with shovels. By 1850 most of the major transport routes had been taken over by the railways and the lot of them were out of a job.

Around 1850 the Corporation were finally successful in draining what remained of the King's Fish Pool. A new road imaginatively called "Foss Islands Road" was made and new railway sidings were built on the reclaimed land. As always with roads, when you build one you suddenly discover that you need more and more of them. Some natural law that the authorities haven't discovered yet, must exist that says new roads do not eliminate traffic congestion, they only add to it. The more new roads you have, the more people use them and thus increase traffic flow on other roads leading to the new road. So you need other new roads to help increase the traffic flow to the other roads that are becoming more congested due to traffic using any way they can to get to where they want to go........phew! No wonder that no one has ever been able to come up with an integrated transport policy, and don't forget we are still talking about a period before the automobile - just!

The city became congested, not only that, but people living and working on the opposite sides of the river wanted a more direct access to the station. It was bloody frustrating if you lived in Marygate, just across the river from the station, but had to drive your cart all the way through town, cross over Ouse Bridge and all the way up to Toft Green, just to get to a point that you could have swum in ten minutes, providing you could swim, and that the nasty currents and effluent didn't get you first.

Throughout the early half of the 1800's large numbers of proposals to build a second bridge nearer to the station were considered, um'd and ah'd over for a while, shelved, taken out again, re-examined, filed, and finally, in 1857, decided upon.

The site decided on for this new bridge was between Lendal Tower, home of the waterworks, and Barker Tower, the home of the man who operated a ferry between these points. It doesn't take much imagination to realise how upset he must have been by the news. At first he ranted and raved, then concentrated on writing letters to the press, then sulked when they didn't get printed. Finally he took direct action. He went on strike! Now that may seem a bit of a daft thing to do at first, that is until you realise that bridges take some time to build, how would people get across in that time. His militant actions worked, and when the bridge was finally built, he received a lump of cash, a was given a free horse and cart, and sent on his way.

Mind you building bridges wasn't as easy as it first seemed. The bridge at Lendal was completed in 1860, but unfortunately in the following year it collapsed killing five people. The remains were hauled out of the river, an action that seemed very appropriate given that the engineer who built the ill fated structure in the first place went by the name of Dredge!

A new bridge was constructed by a different engineer called Thomas Page and the second Lendal Bridge was finally opened in 1863. Mind you the council did all right out of the salvage operations. They sold the remains of the first bridge to Scarborough Council who used them to build the infamous Valley Bridge, which incidentally is still standing.

Of course the new bridge had to lead somewhere and so new holes were created in the city wall that created the road that now leads to the railway station, with a second route, Leeman Road, being tunnelled under the railway lines heading west out of the city.

It was only a matter of time until the people who lived at the opposite end of the city wanted a bridge of their own and so in 1881 another bridge was built on the site of another ferry that crossed the Ouse between Skeldergate Postern and York Castle. Again another ferry man was sent on his way a happy man.

The construction of Skeldergate Bridge almost completed a circular route around the walled city, which was finally accomplished by the building of Castle Mills Bridge, and Layerthorpe Bridge both crossing the Foss. This early form of "ring road" allowed the city to expand outwards, using the circular route around the walls almost as a hub with expansion carrying on along the "spokes" formed by the roads that lead away from the city.

With people living further away from the center of the city a phenomena began to appear, that of the commuter. It really began in 1835 when horse drawn buses were first seen on the city streets. These were taken over in 1880 by the York Tramway Company who introduced steam driven and eventually electric powered trams. They first ran a service from Fulford to Castle Mills Bridge, which was extended to Clifford Street and then across Ouse Bridge, up Micklegate to the Mount where the route terminated at the corner of Dalton Terrace. Going up Micklegate hill proved very difficult and even after the introduction of steam and electric, horses still had to be used to pull the vehicle successfully up the hill.

Despite the difficulties of manoeuvering through York's narrow streets, trams were one of the great ideas of the last century. They moved people around, not only in York but in many other British cities, in a really cost effective and environmentally friendly manner. The worst thing that could happen with trams was that, towards the end of the century when the bicycle became popular, many of the towns cyclists would get their wheels caught in the tram rails and end up having to cycle miles out of their way until they reached the terminus or until a kind person pushed them over. This latter method was discouraged however as over enthusiastic helpers and small children would derive great sadistic enjoyment from pushing cyclists over whether they were stuck in tram rails or not.

The one place not to get your wheel stuck was at the top of Micklegate. Once trapped there it was, literally, downhill all the way to Ouse Bridge. Such was the danger of this route that the council placed small sand traps alongside the tram rails that in theory would slow the out of control cyclists down. In actuality all they did was to attract large numbers of the city's cat population who suddenly thought that the Council had provided numbers of excellent cat litter trays.

Other developments and civic improvements brought York to the doorstep of the twentieth century. For better or worse, in 1878 the first telephone arrived in York. A day later the first wrong number was dialled and three days later the first heavy breather was arrested. It took a week before a double glazing company made the first uninvited telesales call.

The following years saw the building of the City Art Gallery, new Council Chambers and Council Offices next to the Guildhall, and a Public Library. New law courts, a police station, and fire station were built in the newly created Clifford Street.. In 1884 The General Post Office was built in Lendal. If you ever bother to look up at the upper floors you'll see some really fine art deco lettering and leaded windows that seem to be influenced by the great Scottish architect, raincoat manufacturer and inventor of digestive tablets, Charles Rennie Mackintosh.

As the century prepared to change the first automobile rattled its way through the city. Despite these new transport improvements, river transport was still important to the city and many of the raw materials needed by York's new industries were brought into the city by barge. Wheat was brought up to Wormalds Cut where new flour mills built by Henry Leetham were opened in 1861, but the main river goods went to supply York's other growing industry, chocolate and sweet manufacture.

Remember in the last chapter when I wrote "more of them later"? Well this is later! The successors to Mary Tuke's small business were now operating a small factory grinding cocoa and chicory and producing a type of chocolate. The chocolate side of the business was then sold to Isaac Rowntree, the son of another York Grocer In its turn the business passed to Joseph Rowntree who, in 1889, made the decision to purchase some Dutch machinery that enabled him to produce the better tasting chocolate that York and the rest of the world was waiting for. His company soon expanded and he built new factories in Tanner's Moat and North Street, handy for the docks on Queen's Staithe, and for the railway which ran a couple of sidings down from the station.

Products manufactured by Rowntrees hit a nation that discovered it had a very sweet tooth, especially when boxes of chocolates became the fashionable thing to give as a romantic gesture, usually accompanied by a large ribbon, a bunch of flowers and a little note saying "Sorry!"

To cope with increased demands for chocolate products the factory moved to Haxby Road, to the north of the City, and in 1879 employed around a hundred workers. In 1897 it employed a thousand people and by 1910 the figure had grown to over four thousand.

Terry's also were doing very well for themselves, they were busy manufacturing marmalade, cakes, comfits, candied peel, medicated lozenges, and sugar based sweets like sugar mice, barley sugar, and cough candy. In 1886 they began to produce chocolate products, and at the turn of the century, introduced the first ever boxed chocolate assortment

They also discovered that most essential part of anybody's Christmas festivities, the Terry's Chocolate Orange. They moved their manufacturing base from the back of the small shop in St. Helen's Square to Clementhorpe, and eventually out to its present site at the back of the racecourse.

There is another sweet manufacturer in York, Cravens, best remembered for the catch phrase from the 1950's and 60's that went "The Best English Mint, mm, mm." The company was founded by Mary Ann Craven who inherited two small shops and then switched to the manufacture of sweets, specialising at the mintier end of the market.

The sudden availability of jobs led to an increase in York's population. At the start of the nineteenth century around 17,000 people lived in the city. That figure grew to 28,000 by the middle of the century and by 1850 it shot up to 40,000. By the time the First World War came along that figure had doubled.

But where did all these people come from? Well up to 1840 most of the city's incomers were from the agricultural areas of the North Riding. Let's face it, the new jobs offered by York's new offices, workshops and factories were infinitely better than the poverty being experienced by the agricultural labourers. At least you were inside, dry, and had a slightly wider choice of food than turnips everyday!

After 1840 the City became a magnet for incomers from the West Riding towns, and Irish immigrants escaping the famine that spread through their own country. In ten years the numbers of Irish living in York increased from around three hundred to nearly two thousand. The majority of this large Irish community settled in the Bedern and around the Walmgate areas of York and brought with them their own rich Irish culture and heritage. It would be very interesting to know what they would have made of today's new trend in the creation of Irish Theme pubs that's spreading through the city. Would they recognise their own heritage if they ventured for a pint into somewhere called "Scruffy Herbert's" selling heavily gassed, "genuine Irish Beer and Porter", whilst a group of English folk musicians sit in the corner hammering out their version of "The Rocky Road to Dublin" and other hits from the Val Doonican and Van Morrison Irish Book of Songs? Probably not is the answer.

The down side of this population expansion was that everyone needed somewhere to live. Soon small low cost houses were built on the land that was originally the gardens of the earlier Georgian buildings. Soon small networks of courtyards and alleyways filled up any available space until the city was packed tight. Inside these small dwellings the people were packed in even tighter.

The larger Georgian mansions and town houses owned by wealthy York families who, having made their money, had moved to larger houses either in the country or in London, had been converted into workshops and rented rooms in which the poor were packed in like so many sardines.

Whatever you do, never, never mistake the quaint pseudo Victorian images you find on Christmas cards and old paintings, as the real thing. This mythology of the "Good Old Days" is endorsed by reproduction Victorian streets in theme parks, and recreated streets built in museums whose curators should know better.

Whilst one cannot knock the popular success of the reproduction Victoria and Edwardian streets to be seen in York's Castle Museum, one does feel that the sterile atmosphere doesn't really convey the real deprivation that the city experienced during this period. Although various elements of the city and its trades are adequately represented, the general impression that a visitor takes away with them is one of warmth and cosines, the very antithesis of the harsh reality of Victorian York.

For a start these streets are so clean you can eat your pre-packed lunch from them. If we really want a true representation of a Victorian street there should, at the very least, be piles of horse droppings scattered about the place. As well as the cute little stuffed sparrows there should be some cute little stuffed rats, preferably suffering from rickets, scuttling about the place. The place shouldn't just smell bad, it should reek of the unique, heady mixture of soot, smoke, river sewage, and rotting garbage. In fact the entire atmosphere should recreated by false smoke and smog drifting about and there should be at least an inch thick covering of black soot on all the roofs and window sills.

If you really want to know what life was like for the Victorian working classes read your Charles Dickens, your Mayhew and your William Cobbett. Forget the pretty paintings of Atkinson Grimshaw, check out the works of Dore. Just in case you still don't get the picture let me tell you straight. The living conditions experienced by the Victorian poor were atrocious. They were appalling, detestable, execrable, horrible, horrifying, shocking, and terrible. The people suffered from numerous health problems created by bad sewerage and drainage, bad water, and bad air. They suffered from working in dark, damp, cramped, workshops that today would drive a deaf, dumb and blind health and safety officer instantly insane.

Despite the city appointing its first medical officer of health, a year after the government had passed the Public Health Act of 1872, the sanitation was sparse. Someone with a nose for figures once worked out that somewhere in the small streets and courtyards were eight thousand earth toilets, pleasantly known as middens, each being used by anything from four to fourteen different families! Even when buildings had the luxury of sewers they were so unreliable that every time the river flooded the sewers would flow backwards and the cellars would fill up with ripe, raw sewage. By the turn of the century still only forty percent of York's houses had a toilet they could call their own.

Given these facts it should come as no surprise to know that disease was rampant. Due to the cramped living conditions, if someone in one house caught a cold, within the hour it would have spread at least three streets away. Unfortunately colds were the least of their problems. Influenza, typhus, TB, dysentery, and cholera were just some of the killers that stalked the city like a tall skeleton holding a scythe, SPEAKING IN CAPITAL LETTERS, and dressed in a black hooded cloak.

One of the worst outbreaks of cholera occurred in 1832 in Skeldergate in an area laughingly known as "Hagworm Nest" and claimed 200 lives. A special graveyard was built outside the city walls part of which can still be seen across the road from the station. A nice welcoming site for new arrivals and eager tourists! In 1847 an outbreak of typhus swept through the Walmgate area and also claimed many lives.

As an illustration of just how bad conditions really were, think about this - in 1770 the life expectancy of a York resident was 28 years of age. In 1801 it had crept up to 29, and by 1841 it had reached the grand old age of 32! Now as we all know statistics can say many things. These figures don't mean that, in 1841, as soon as you reached 32 you popped your clogs. They mean that a lot of people died young, very young. In 1770 thirty eight per cent of all deaths in the city were those of children aged under five. In the 1801 figures this tender age group account for thirty five percent, and in 1841 a staggering forty two percent when almost half the deaths in the city were suffered by under five year olds. In the 1880's one third of all children born in the Walmgate area died before they were one year old.

Worse areas of deprivation were to be found in the areas of Water Lanes, the small streets that led from Castlegate down to the riverside at King's Staith. As far back as 1818 these streets were being described as housing the "poorest and the most disorderly part of the population". They were eventually demolished when improvements were made to King's Staith in 1851, and when Clifford Street was created in 1881.

Another area notorious for poverty and disease was The Bedern, the old courtyard belonging to the College of Vicars Choral of the Minster, which by the 1840's has fallen into such decline that entire area was flattened, cleared of slum housing, and converted into a thoroughfare.

Meanwhile across the river new working class housing was being created on land originally belonging to the Holy Trinity Priory and on land where the Mansion of the Duke of Buckingham had been demolished when the bloke went belly up at the end of the seventeenth century. Priory Street was created in 1854 and the area known as Bishophill became built up between 1851 and 1871. A new entrance in the city wall called Victoria Bar had been created in 1840 connecting Bishophill with Nunnery Lane and housing continued to develop in the new streets beyond. In fact in the period between 1830 and 1860 in various parts of the city around two hundred houses a year were built. Boom time once again for the building trade and for the sellers of red lamps and rope.

There are in existence a number of photographs taken in the Bedern and Walmgate areas of the city that show the real face of Victorian York. It would be nice if such institutions as the Castle Museum put these on display to show visitors what the city was really like for its many occupants. In my humble opinion, if you're going to lay claims to being "England's most popular museum of everyday life", it would be nice to show what everyday life was really like. For God's sake tell it like it was! If not, if you're going out to create a false, Mary Poppins like myth, then get yourself sponsored by the Disney Corporation. There's no shame in telling the truth, in fact some places like the Eden Camp Museum at Malton and the Museum of Embarkation in Liverpool's Maritime Museum, positively benefit from telling it like it really was. As a people we need to know what really happened. We've long since grown up, and no longer need our historical facts to be clouded by an arm of protectivisim.

The world that the museum shuns is the real world in which, if you're middle aged like me, our Grandparents grew up in. That's our ancestry they're playing with and I for one want to be proud of the fact that my folks came out of that stock, that they gritted their teeth and survived, despite disease, poverty and the rest of the everyday crap they had to put up with.

CHAPTER FOURTEEN

TWENTIETH CENTURY YORK

The beginning of the Twentieth Century saw Britain as the top country in the world, and the birth of the phrase "We're British and we're best". Britannia not only ruled the waves but also most of the available landmasses, and God blessed all who sailed in her. For a brief while Britain was the chosen land, and the English its chosen people, or so it seemed. The country had a stable political system, led the world in technology and industrialisation and sold its many product in the furthest flung corners of the British Empire. Be it in the plains of deepest Africa, the jungles of the Far East, or in the frozen wastelands of Canada, for better or worse, you were never too far away from British made products, policies and attitudes. You could order a tin of Farrah's Harrogate Toffee, a packet of Woodbines, a bottle of Bass and a Cravens "Best English Mint.. mm..mm.." anywhere in the world and be pretty sure that they would turn up - eventually.

But despite this apparent wealth, when you scratched the surface of society, underneath nothing had really changed. As always the rich were getting richer and the poor were getting poorer. That sounds familiar doesn't it! As I've already said, history tends to repeat itself, and despite political changes, civil wars, invasions, inventions, growing parliamentary power, riots, loonies and other general disruptions, the one constant thing throughout over 2000 years of English history is that the rich got richer and the poor got the proverbial kick in the balls! Remember the Golden Rule?

At the end of the nineteenth century a book written by Charles Booth for the first time exposed the harsh living conditions experienced by the poor and working class of London. In York, this book shocked Joseph Rowntree's son Seebohm so much that he decided to investigate the living conditions of the people in his own city, many of them working for his own family's company. Between 1899 and 1901

Seebohm, with some helpers, visited over 11,560 York families gaining information as to their income and expenditure.

Seebohm was also determined to discover where the mythical "poverty line" actually was. Bear in mind that for the last hundred years or so discovery had been the name of the game, and all manner of lines had been unearthed. There was the Meridian Line, the Thin Red Line, the P&O Line, the Plimsoll Line, the Northern Line, the Central Line and the East Coast Main Line. Later this century there would be the discovery of the Siegfried Line, the Maginot Line, white lines, double yellow lines, What's My Line?, "above the line" and "below the line", snorting lines, the Rock Island Line, and finally, as we approach the end of the century, a pastime that seems to have got half of Britain into checked shirts and cowboy boots - Line Dancing.

Seebohm discovered the poverty line by working out how much money each family needed to pay for life's basic essentials, and here they didn't mean a car, a fridge, a telly and a video, they meant the real basics, food, fuel, clothes and rent.. After much deliberation he came to the conclusion that a single person needed 7/- (36p) per week, a married couple 11/8 (58p), a family with two children 18/10 (85p), and a family with four children 26/- (£1.30). Of course, for anyone reading this book who was born after the decimalisation of British currency, (Feb. 15th 1971), you've probably no idea what 7/- means. You've also got no idea of what a con trick on the British public decimalisation really proved to be. The government couldn't be seen to devalue the pound so instead they invented a new coinage under cover of which every manufacturer and retailer put their prices up, thinking we wouldn't know how much we were paying anymore.

Boy were they right! Pre-decimalisation it was still possible to have a good night out, buy a packet of cigarettes, drink fifteen pints of fighting bitter, go to the pictures, get a fish supper on the way home and still have change out of a pound note. After decimalisation you needed to take out a mortgage to buy a pint!

But back to the plot - Just in case anyone would accuse Seebohm of being too generous he made a great issue of pointing out the things he didn't classify as essentials. No money could be spent on bus or train fares, no newspapers, no concert going, no letters to be posted, no contributions to a church or chapel, no help or lending money to anyone, no membership fees to be paid to a Trade Union or any sick club, no pocket money given to children, no sweets, no toys, no smoking, no drinking, and everyone in the family could only wear working clothes. They couldn't spend any money on health care, and if they needed medical attention they had to rely on the parish doctor. They were allowed no time off work ill and, if they died, they had to buried by the parish. Now that doesn't sounds too generous does it!

Seebohm published his book "Poverty, A Study of Town Life." in 1901. For once and for all it lifted the veil from the facade of the so called wealthy society. It showed that, in York, one thousand four hundred and sixty five families lived under the poverty line, nearly ten per cent of the total population.

The book also blew apart the myth perpetuated by the wealthier and more privileged classes who claimed that the poor were all work-shy, drunken slobs, that didn't want to work, and therefore it was their own fault they were poor. I've a feeling that the very same thoughts made by the very same type of people have been said throughout the century and are still being said today. Somewhere in the not too distant past I seem to remember someone in authority claiming that all unemployment would be solved if only we got on our bicycles.

Seebohm's book pointed out that half the people under the poverty line were there despite the fact that the husband was in regular employment, and his wife was efficient in running the house. Finally he made himself really popular among the York company owners and company directors by pin pointing the cause of poverty as low wages, coupled with the lack of sickness and unemployment benefits.

Rowntree's book goes on to detail the expenditure of eighteen different families and, if you go in for reading that sort of stuff, is well worth browsing through. It gives us a very detailed description and unique insight into the sort of life the ordinary York person lived almost

100 years ago to the day. Read that and you realise just how inept the phrase "The Good Old Days" really is.

The book also shows that people have always lived just a sixpence in excess of what they earned. Dickens never wrote a truer word in his life when he put these words into the mouth of Mr. Micawber -

"Annual income twenty pound, annual expenditure nineteen pounds nineteen and six, result happiness. Annual income twenty pounds, annual expenditure twenty pounds and sixpence, result misery."

Of course in Dickens' day they didn't have the benefits of credit cards, cash points, bonus points, loyalty cards, mail order catalogues, coupons, money saving offers via direct mail and all the other things that conspire in our lives today to ensure that, no matter how much we earn, the availability of easy credit will always enable us to spend more than we earn. It seems as if the fate of mankind is to spend money we haven't got, buying things we don't really need and don't really want in the first place.

The effect of Rowntree's book had far reaching effects, and not just in York. Throughout Britain it swayed public opinion and even had an effect on the ruling Liberal Party, especially on two politicians called Asquith and Lloyd George (who, incidentally knew my father), who fought for, and eventually established, the beginnings of the welfare state.

The Rowntree family themselves acted as great public benefactors. Joseph Rowntree founded his Village Trust and, inspired by the ideas of one Ebenezer Howard, began to construct the first ever "garden village". It was built on the outskirts of the city within easy reach of Rowntree's factory, and was called New Earswick. The village contained cottage type houses complete with gardens, set within pleasant, tree lined streets. The village also contained community facilities such as a folk hall and a primary school. After it's success New Earswick formed the basic plan for the later new towns of Welwyn Garden City, Leitchworth and ultimately Milton Keynes, although

Rowntree himself drew the line at putting herds of concrete cows in the surrounding fields.

As well as being the first "garden village" New Earswick is also famous for an event that happened during the late 1960's. You will find that whenever you are in the presence of York residents who managed to live through the psychedelic 60's and remember them, they will speak in whispers of the legendary gig played in New Earswick folk hall by The Pink Floyd. Yes that's THE Pink Floyd, the original line up complete with Syd Barrett, just before their record "Arnold Layne" climbed into the lower echelons of the charts. In the course of much research and a lot of drinking I have spoken to people who claimed that they were actually there! I wonder if, years from now, people who were at the local gigs of Shed Seven will look back on them with such deep rooted nostalgia?

Although the two events were unconnected, just as Seebohm Rowntree published his book, Queen Victoria died and the country passed from the Victorian Age into a new era of extravagant enjoyments known as the Edwardian Period, obviously named after the new King, yet another Edward, the seventh in fact.

Edward was over 60 years of age when he eventually came to the throne and, due to Queen Victoria's slightly biased opinion that he was a weak and irresponsible sort of bloke, she had kept him well out of the way of state affairs. This opinion was partially due to her belief that her son's scandalous behavior had been a contributory factor in the death of Prince Albert. Mind you, Edward did, almost single handedly, invent ladism well before the 1990's. He loved horse racing, shooting, golf, women, croquet, cards, motoring, sailing, wine, more women and song. In fact when it came to woman and song he usually preferred the two together, having counted among his many mistresses both Lillie Langtry and Sarah Bernhardt.

Edward's Coronation in 1902 heralded a new age. The Boer War ended, Victorian attitudes were dying off, and the Yorkshire County Cricket team were county champions. God was in his heaven and all was well in the British Empire. The country acted like middle aged woman just released from a very tight corset, - it let it's hair down and began to enjoy itself. Music halls sprung up, and "variety" was born. Soon hordes of jugglers, singers, acrobats, exotic dancers, comedians, and male and female impersonators were traveling the length and breath of Britain doing their turns somewhere on the bill. Then, just as quickly, the music hall was replaced by the electronic moving picture house, cinema to you and me. The remains of one of York's earliest cinemas can still be seen in Fossgate, where it's elaborate archway frames the entrance to McDonalds. No, not the place to go in York for a quarter pounder with cheese, fries and a shake, it's a furniture shop.

For a while the York cinemas and music halls lived side by side. In York, before the First World War it was possible to see a matinee movie at "The Picture House" in Coney Street and then pop down to Clifford Street to see a live evening show at the Empire Theatre. Other cinemas in York were the Rialto, the Grand on Clarence Street, the Tower in New Street and later, one in Fishergate, the ABC on Blossom Street and the Clifton.

In 1909 York Corporation took over the running of the city's trams and it was their turn to face the problems of getting the things through the narrow streets, up Micklegate Hill and through the bar entrance. In 1915 they introduced petrol buses which, over the next twenty years, gradually replaced the trams. They finally stopped running in 1934 when the Corporation made an arrangement with the West Yorkshire Road Car Company to jointly run York's public road transport. Other York based bus services were run by the Yorkshire Pullman company.

Incidentally, for what it's worth, my own favourite York buses were blue ones, run by a company called East Yorkshire and had funny rounded tops, making them look a bit egg shaped. Evidently they were made this way to go under the medieval bar entrance to Beverley. An ingenious solution to the old problem of how to get a fourteen foot high bus through a ten foot nine inch high archway.

In 1908 the largest political demonstration ever seen in Britain was held in London's Hyde Park where half a million people gathered to celebrate "Women's Sunday" and to listen to speaker after speaker demanding the right for women to be given the vote. This large scale protest was the culmination of events first started back in 1903 by Emmeline Pankhurst and her two daughters Christabel and Sylvia who together founded the Women's Social and Political Union.

Up to 1908 the protests of the W.S.P.U. had largely been confined to heckling politicians (a worth while hobby for anyone to take up), for which the protesters were usually carted away and arrested. Despite the success of the Hyde Park demonstration Asquith, the Liberal Prime Minister, still refused the demands of the suffragettes. The protesters were left with no option but to change tactics and become more militant and more aggressive.

In London protesters broke the windows of 10 Downing Street. They tried to storm the house of Parliament, and they chained themselves to railings. The militancy spread and soon, throughout the entire country, politicians were having eggs and stones thrown at them, windows were being broken, letter boxes set on fire, and women chained themselves to railings. Hundreds of protesters were arrested and thrown into prison where, to support their demands to be treated as political prisoners and not criminals, they went on hunger strike.

The authorities, in a desperate attempt to stop the protesters gaining public sympathy, carried out a policy of force feeding them. Unfortunately the plan backfired. The force feeding was done under such barbaric circumstances that the hunger strikers immediately gained the public's sympathy! Then the government tried a new policy, one called "cat and mouse", where they released the hunger strikers only to re-arrest them after they had been out in the outside world a for a few days and had a good meal.

The first martyr of the suffragette cause was a woman called Emily Davison who, during the 1913 Derby, threw herself at the King's horse. The horse fell and knocked her down. Four days later she died of her injuries. Her funeral was the last great gathering of the suffragette movement, for despite their militancy continuing, greater global events overtook the domestic issue. On the outbreak of the First World War, at the request of the government, Mrs. Pankhurst agreed to suspend all forms of protest. When peace eventually returned the suffragettes were rewarded. The government finally granted the vote to women aged over thirty. Ten years later the vote was given to all men and women over the age of twenty one.

In the same year a music hall artist called Florrie Forde began singing a song about an Irish immigrant in London. It was called "It's a long way to Tipperary". However the original meaning of the lyrics was soon to be lost as, in 1914 the song took on a very different meaning when it became the theme song for the greatest and most tragic event of the first half of the twentieth century, The First World War which touched just about every household, not just in York, but throughout the country.

It must have been a strange feeling to experience the summer of 1914, one minute it was party, party, party, the next it was "pack up your troubles in your old kit bag." On 28th June 1914 few people bothered to read a story about the assassination of Archduke Franz Ferdinand and his wife in the small Balkan town of Sarajevo, but just over a month later Austria, France, Russia and Germany were all at war with each other.

In the first days of August the mood in Britain was a desire for peace, but a under the Entente Cordiale agreement of 1904, the government was honour bound to assist the French. The Liberal government was deeply divided, some ministers threatened to resign if Britain went to war whilst others threatened to resign if they didn't. The government was finally pushed off the fence by the action of the Germans, who made France's elaborate defences totally ineffective by simply walking around them. Unfortunately for all concerned this walk took them through Belgium, and under a treaty signed in 1839, Britain was a guarantor of Belgian neutrality. The government chose to honour this treaty and, at 11pm on August 1914, the First World War officially kicked off.

On Dec. 16th German warships sailed along the East Coast shelling Hartlepool, Whitby, and Scarborough. This event led to demands for more defence and the Royal Naval Air Service established airship sub-stations along the coast. However the following year the Germans launched a series of Zeppelin raids. This action prompted the Royal Flying Corps to take over the aerial defence of the country and they established airfields on many racecourses, including one on York's Knavesmire that became home to 33 Squadron. On 2nd and 3rd of May 1916 York was attacked by an enemy for the first time since the Civil War when Zeppelin L-21 dropped a number of bombs on the city. After this attack York residents demanded that the airfield should be moved away from the city and it moved to Copmanthorpe.

When war had been formally declared and the British Expeditionary Force set off for France, the word on the street was that it would be all over by Christmas. The word was wrong! It took almost a year for the British Government to realise one awful, very important fact, that Imperial Germany was a damn sight stronger than they had imagined. In the summer of 1915 they finally reacted and established new manufacturing and munitions factories, and ushered in a revolutionary concept, the mass employment of a female workforce. Suddenly women were working in shipyards, in factories, in offices, and proving both as valuable and as effective as any male workforce

The war dragged on for another three years until, after a series of Allied victories, starting with the winning of the Second Battle of the Somme, Germany finally asked the President of the United States to broker a peace treaty. The armistice was signed on November 11th 1918.

After the celebrations had died down and everyone had finally managed to shake of their hangovers, the country settled down and tried to get back on an even keel. Decent housing became a priority and The Housing Act of 1919 made government subsidies available to city councils and corporations for house building.

To some extent York had already begun to address this issue. Earlier, in 1915 York Corporation had bought the area of land known as Tang Hall, and had began to build a major development that covered some 288 acres, creating York's first council houses. Between 1919 and

1939 York Council demolished nearly 2,000 sub standard houses, mainly in the areas of Walmgate, Layerthorpe, Navigation Road and Hungate, and built around 5,000 new houses. Land in Acomb was developed and, in the late 1920's, the Holgate and Burton Stone Lane areas of York were also developed.

The same period also saw a large growth in employment. In 1911 it is estimated that the confectionery industry led by Rowntrees and Terry's employed around three and a half thousand people, by 1939 they employed over twelve thousand, almost thirty per cent of York's total workforce whilst the railways employed a further thirteen per cent.

In 1927 a sugar factory, was built just off the Boroughbridge Road, in Acomb and ever since, during sugar beet season, the residents of York have become accustomed to driving in long queues of traffic stuck behind tractors pulling great wagon loads of sugar beet. One of the things you learn very quickly as a newcomer to the city is never, ever follow these wagons too closely. Many have been the dented car bonnets and smashed windscreens as sugar beets the size and constituency of cannon balls bounce, roll and catapult from the backs of these overfilled wagons. Today York residents can always tell which direction the wind is blowing by the mysterious sickly sweet smell that drifts across the city emanating from the sugar factory. Still, it's a hell of an improvement on the smells of the medieval city.

Mind you, between the wars the smell of the city must have been pretty ripe just outside Walmgate where the cattle market was still situated. The market provided part time employment for many in the Walmgate area, but the favourite job of the period was that of "bullock-walloper". This job was as simple and descriptive as it sounded. Armed with a large stick all the bloke had to do was to keep the cattle in order for the fat market on Tuesdays. There were almost one hundred and fifty men employed, they would wait for the trains to bring the cattle to Foss Islands Road and once unloaded would drive the beasts out into the surrounding fields and then drive them back again in time for the market. During this period it must have been impossible for motorists to drive up Hull Road with thousands of cattle heading in the opposite direction, blocking up the road. God only knows what happened to all the resulting manure, but in the gardens of many houses along Hull Road are traces of once great rose bushes.

The Town Planning Act of 1925 required all British cities with a population of over 20,000 to undertake town planning studies and prepare schemes for future growth and York Council responded by planning a ring road around the city. The plan stated that the new road would cross the Ouse at Clifton and form a circular route, linking up all the major routes in and out of the city The first bit of the scheme was the construction of a duel carriageway at Kingsway in 1929, but then the council did a U-turn and canceled the project altogether.

Strange as it may seem today, only seventy odd years ago this same town planning act also called for each town to have it's own airport. York chose to built one on Clifton Moor, however the fashion for civic airports soon fell out of favour and by 1938 the aerodrome had reverted to a private flying club, with a fleet of seven aircraft. However in the next few years the aerodrome would prove to play a vital part in the defence of the country.

In May 1926, the T.U.C. called for industrial action to support the miners who had been arguing with the pit owners for almost a year. The owners had come up with a great idea to sustain their profits by demanding shorter working hours at a reduced rate. Surprisingly enough the miners had told them what to do with their great idea. In retaliation for the miners making up the catchy slogan "Not a penny off the pay - Not a minute off the day" the owners locked them out of their work.

The support the T.U.C. received was overwhelming. From midnight on May 3rd over 2 million workers, ninety per cent of the total workforce downed tools. Dockers, power workers, transport workers, printers, shipbuilders, and even copper bottom clinker scrapers and their mates, went on strike for nine days. The government called for volunteers to man the wheels of industry and many people willingly left their desk bound jobs to dabble in more exciting industries. Throughout the country students took over the buses, a situation that led to some bizarre occurrences, especially considering that no one actually knew the routes the buses were meant to travel on. For the passengers it was nine exciting days of travel by Russian Roulette. The destination numbers and names meant nothing. If a bus came along you caught it. If it went anywhere near where you wanted to go, it was a bonus. Legend among York bus drivers claims that such a bus set out on at three p.m. May 7th to travel from York to Acomb. It missed the turn off at Holgate Road and carried on down the A64, never to be seen again. For many years whispered sightings claimed that the bus had been seen in such places as Leeds, Peterborough and even in London itself. One person even claimed they had seen it in 1962 packed with clean, healthy looking young people all heading for a Summer Holiday.

At the turn of the century York Prison had been closed for civil offenders and was handed over to the military to be used as a detention barracks, until 1929 when it finally closed altogether. The building and the entire site was purchased by York City Council in 1934 who immediately demolished the 19th century prison building and the great surrounding wall, revealing Clifford's Tower once again. As it had been walled up for well over a hundred years most of York's inhabitants didn't know it was there. When the walls were knocked down, crowds gathered staring at the strange building that had suddenly appeared in the centre of town. However they didn't get much of a chance to explore it. No sooner was it revealed than it was declared an important historic building and a turnstile and admittance charge was placed across its doorway.

In 1938 the building known as the Female Prison was opened as a museum housing a huge cornucopia of bits and pieces of folk life collected by Dr. James Kirk, who boldly collected where no man had collected before. Dr. Kirk was a doctor who travelled around the countryside treating people and collecting bits and pieces of bric-a-brac. He realised that, as the years passed, a way of life was disappearing before his very eyes, so he collected everything he could. Dr. Kirk didn't just collect small items like kitchen utensils, Valentine cards, ornaments and policemen's truncheons, he went the whole way and collected large things like fire engines, Hansom cabs, and entire timber framed buildings.

Eventually when he had filled up his own house, a gypsy caravan that he had collected, four garden sheds and his garage, his wife eventually put her foot down. In 1935 he gave the lot to the City of York, who had more spare sheds than he did. Eventually, when the female prison became free they put the lot on display and opened it up to the general public. It was from those beginnings that the Castle Museum we all know and love today was spawned.

On Saturday 2nd September 1939 in Football Division Three (Northern) York City were beaten 1-0 away from home by Rochdale - nothing new there! The following morning, as he was halfway through reading his sermon Dr. Temple, the Archbishop of York took a note from his verger. He then told the congregation gathered inside York Minster that Britain was at war with Germany. Those who hadn't been at the Minster had tuned in radios at 11.15am to hear Neville Chamberlain, the Prime Minister, declare to the nation that Britain had been at war for the last 15 minutes.

On the outbreak of war York's aerodrome was taken over by the R.A.F. At first it was used only as a satellite station by R.A.F. Linton but, by the end of the year, it had been taken over by the Army Co-operation Command. In the August of 1940 Lysander aircraft from 4 Squadron, Royal Air Force had taken residence.

Obviously the major event in York during the Second World War was the Blitz that occurred on the night of 29th April 1942. It was around midnight that the air-raid sirens sounded their warning and a few minutes later flares began to light up the City. A York newspaper stated that

> *"Showers of incendiaries were dropped, followed by high explosives and the raiders dived and machine gunned blazing buildings and streets."*

Soon fires broke out all over town. The railway station was hit, as were the marshalling yards at Leeman Road, the Bar Convent, and a number of houses, but the greatest damage was the destruction of two of York's oldest buildings, the church of St. Mary-Le-Grand in Coney

Street and the ancient Guildhall. Fortunately just before the war the valuable medieval stained glass had been removed from the church, but unfortunately a major renovation scheme to the Guildhall was just nearing completion when the building was gutted. York Airfield was also hit, the guard room receiving a direct hit killing everyone inside it. Other severe damage was done to the airfield, hangers, and buildings, and the officers mess.

Many people thought that the true German target had been the Minster and that the raid had been a so-called Baedeker Raid in reprisal for the British bombing of the historic German city of Cologne. However this theory proved untrue. After the war among many captured German documents were maps of York on which were marked the railway station, marshalling yards, Lendal Bridge and the electricity station.

If you can get hold of it there's an interesting book about the York blitz, called surprisingly enough, York Blitz. The author went to great lengths in his research, even managing to track down a German bomb aimer who took part in the raid. He is quoted as saying that his plane was one of the last of the raiders and in the distance he could see fires already blazing at the selected targets. As he took aim a factory appeared in his sights and his thumb twitched. At the last minute he decided against dropping his load on the factory and instead dropped them on the pre-arranged target. It was later revealed that the factory he saw had been Rowntrees. Not much danger in blowing up a chocolate factory, or so you would think. However unknown to many people, especially the Germans, as well as manufacturing chocolate, Rowntrees factory was also manufacturing munitions. It is quiet possible that, if the Germans had scored a direct hit, half of York would have been blown off the face of the map. Saved by the twitching thumb of a German Bombardier.

Throughout the war, as well as being home to No 4 Army Co-operation Squadron R.A.F., York airfield also housed the York Aircraft Repair Depot, a factory that was staffed mainly by York women and responsible for the repair of Halifax Bombers. Here badly damaged aircraft were scrapped to provide spare parts whilst salvageable aircraft were repaired and completely overhauled before being sent back into service. At the end of the war the factory was used to scrap over half of Britain's remaining Halifax bombers. One, as it came into the airfield managed to clip the tip of a church spire and crashed onto houses causing some loss of life. It is estimated that at one point in 1945/6 there were certainly over a thousand of these aircraft parked up on the runway. Now that must have been a sight to see, hundreds of Halifax's parked up, waiting for the final cut.

Today the site of York Airfield is lost under the 1980's light industrial and out of town shopping development at Clifton Moor. I think the main runway might have been under Tesco's deli counter, but if you wander around and find the entrance to the Maxiprint establishment you will find a small plinth with a plaque on it commemorating York's airfield.

Oh yes! There is one more clue, a new pub near to Tesco's and the multi screen cinema. When breweries build new pubs there's meant to be a certain amount of research undertaken to give the place an appropriate name. Sometimes the breweries cop out and hold competitions among the people who they hope will be the regulars - and sometimes they get it horribly wrong, like they did with "The Flying Legends". It was a simple mistake, the new pub was on Clifton Moor, the sight of the old York airfield. "Memphis Belle" was the hyped up movie of the moment, so what better than to call the pub "The Memphis Belle"?

Well you could hear the screams of protest from the other side of York, at least from Elvington where aviation experts quickly pointed out that American planes like the "Memphis Belle" never came anywhere near Clifton Moor. What did come were Halifax bombers - lots of them! Hence the justifiable outrage at the suggested name of Memphis Belle. It was pointed out to the brewery in question that Clifton Moor and the Halifax Bomber have an honourable heritage and, in due course, the pub was re-named "The Flying Legends" in honour of the Halifax.

In my opinion, whilst York celebrates it's more ancient past, it would be a nice touch if some sort of heritage centre was created, so that today's residents can appreciate the important part that York and it's women played in the story of the Halifax Bomber. Come to think about it, it would be nice if some National, permanent monument was made to acknowledge the contribution the women of Britain made to the war effort as a whole. Personally I think it's a national shame that the Women's Land Army were never even mentioned at the Armistice memorials held every year at the Cenotaph until 1991, forty six years too late.

The war in Europe displaced millions and among the many people escaping the horrors of Nazi Germany were the Barrett family of singers and fugal horn players that became trapped inside Germany when war broke out, during their European Tour of 1939. The family disguised themselves and spent the first two years of the war dressed as a group of singing nuns before escaping over the mountains into Switzerland by the aid of a mountain guide disguised as Julie Andrews. The family eventually settled in York where, despite being stone cold they felt a bit high and dry. Needing some sort of life support they all formed various musical groups and became very famous. Theirs is a true story of hardship and endeavor that great movies are made of.

Post War York saw the cobwebs brushed off the ropes and red lamps and the start of yet another bout of rebuilding and reshaping, that hasn't really stopped today. On 18th July 1946 the York Civic trust was formed with the intention to -

> *"preserve for the benefit of the public the amenities of the City and neighbourhood, to protect from dilapidation, disfigurement or destruction, buildings and open spaces of beauty or historic interest; to acquire land or buildings for that purpose, to hold or develop them themselves, or to hand them over to the City, or to the Nation; to encourage good design and craftsmanship in new erections and to create new beauty within or without the walls."*

A very worthy ideal! I can only assume that they were all looking the other way when someone erected the building known as Stonebow. I have yet to find any written comment about York and its architecture that doesn't condemn this square concrete building totally out of hand. Still, it is the fate of today's generation to live with the mistakes of the older, and they've made the best of a bad job with the opening of Fibbers, York's greatest live music venue. Today many well known popular musical acts strummed their first tentative chords on that hallowed stage. As well as being the home of up and coming acts it also stages gigs by musicians who are either making their come back appearances or established acts who never went away. Whatever the act the place is well worth a visit. As someone once said "a splendid time is guaranteed for all."

The rebuilding of the Guildhall began in 1958 and two years later on 19th June 1960, the fully renovated building was opened by Her Royal Highness Queen Elizabeth the Queen Mother. That same year official approval was given to the creation of York University, founded in the Elizabethan mansion of Heslington Hall. Exciting new buildings were constructed within a landscaped area that includes lakes. In contrast to the Stonebow, the campus reminds us that not all 1960's architects tripped over their white sticks and were savaged by their guide dogs.

Today the City of York attempts to wear many hats. To the numerous tourists it represents a large scale, living heritage centre, filled with real living, breathing people, exciting buildings and many different attractions. Visitors come from all over the world to wander up and down its medieval streets, and visit the Minster.

Entertained by an army of buskers that range from blues singers to living statues and zombies that suddenly shoot ten feet in the air, visitors walk through pedestrian areas with glazed expressions and fists tightly clenched around their credit cards as they window shop in the many specialist shops that offer a wide and bewildering array of up-market goods, fashions, trinkets and foodstuffs. and buy the increasingly tacky selection of dolls, pottery thimbles, tea towels and other nic-naks that people have to buy in order to prove they were actually there.

There is lot's for the visitor to see, and from just about every period of the City's history. From the Roman remains under the Minster, bits of Roman Walls and the Roman Baths under a pub, to the remains of a Norman House. From medieval buildings like Lady Row and the Shambles, to the elegant Georgian houses and mansions, and some great examples of Victoriana. In fact, at the last count in 1988, York contained some 1,530 listed buildings inside the city walls. (I wonder just who the hell it is that keeps counting up such useless information, and who pays them to do it.).

There are numerous attractions to visit such as museums, visitor centers, wax works, railway engines, religious artifacts, reproduction Viking houses, walks around the walls, art & photographic galleries for them to enjoy. They can ride around the city in open topped buses or in horse drawn carriages. They can travel up and down the river drinking in the bars of the splendid river boats, or in rowing boats. They can even get a lift to the National Railway Museum in a bizarre railbus that owes more to Disneyland than to the depository of some of the finest feats of engineering this country has ever produced.

In case the tourists get hungry all the attractions are supported by a wide variety of restaurants, wine bars, cafes, tea rooms, cafe bars, and fast food outlets, and York's specialty, the good value, all day breakfast.

York has some the finest pubs anyone could ever wish for and, as well as offering a wide and wonderful selection of real ales and other alcoholic beverages, offer a wide variety of decor and atmosphere. From the high tech approach of Bruebakers to the 50's charm of the Blue Bell Inn, to a pint inside the Black Swan, the old coaching inn, at Peasholm Green, all tastes are adequately catered for. Although, in addition to members of The Campaign For Real Ale (CAMERA), and its many regulars, I feel that we should call the council to task for allowing the demolishing of The John Bull in Layerthorpe. That pub, virtually untouched since the last war, provided an unique atmosphere, and is sadly missed.

To its many residents, York is a city in which they live and work, and therefore look to it to provide different needs. Mainly it has to maintain an infrastructure of manufacturing and service companies and, in recent years, some major organisations and companies have established or strengthened their presence in the city. Unfortunately many of York's traditional companies have either disappeared or have been taken over and run by faceless managements in boardrooms many miles away from the city. Recently I had occasion to speak to the public relations person in connection with Terry's. I eventually tracked him down in Brussels, in the European Head Office of the American company Philip Morris. Rowntrees have been taken over by the Swiss company Nestle, whose head office is in Croydon, What remains of York's railway industry has just been revived and saved from oblivion by an American Company called Thrall Europa and Ben Johnson's the Printers is now part of R.R.Donnelley & Sons Company, the largest printing organisation in the world, which is run from America.

However some family owned, local rooted businesses are also flourishing. The Shepherd Group seem to be rebuilding Britain single handedly whilst their other family owned company, Portakabin, builders of portable buildings, offices and Roman forts, go from strength to strength.

In addition to their 1950's style offices, General Accident are responsible for the impressive new building that stands by Lendal bridge overlooking the river. All things considered it could have looked a looked a lot worse. If only something could be done with the two ugly office blocks at the bottom of Piccadilly, Ryedale House and United House. Two of the worst examples of modern architecture, and in their way, as bad as Stonebow.

Thanks to the construction of a new bridge across the Ouse, the city is now circled by the ring road which links up to the A64, the main road in and out of the city. Around the Ring Road new light industrial and shopping developments continue to be built. Spreading the city outwards in every direction

York also has to supply entertainment to its residents and its visitors alike. The new Barbican building provides a venue for nationally known acts, whilst the Theatre, complete with its modern facade built in 1967, still struggles on, continuing a tradition founded in 1744. As I write this York City, ably managed by Alan Little are moving up and down the top ten of the second division, when this book comes out will they make it to the First Division? It would be nice to think so. The racecourse is still one of the most popular in Britain. Its original grandstand is now dwarfed between larger and more modern buildings, guaranteed to provide hospitality and good vantage points from which to watch your last tenner disappear in the opposite direction.

Today a visitor can sit at the table of many numerous cafe bars and watch the daily life of York and it's citizens pass by. Sitting there during the day, sipping your coffee and enjoying your all-day breakfast, you can catch a glimpse of famous and infamous York folk as they go on their way. You can sit there with your fried egg sandwich and never realise that you are passing your time with singers, musicians, poets, writers, artists and drinkers whose names will soon be famous across Britain. Well you can never tell. The York band Shed Seven have had a number of major chart hits and are about to undertake a major British tour. For one talented York busker 1997 saw the end of performances in Woolworth's shop doorway and hello to the main stage of Glastonbury when he became a member of The Seahorses - proving there is hope for all of us.

Also, thanks to the existence of an ancient bye-law granted by a Viking King named Hairybendilegges, York is one of the few cities in Britain where you are guaranteed never to be plagued by the scourge of all historic towns, Morris Dancers! To this day, within the City Walls, it is still legal to shoot the daft buggers on sight, providing its done by moonlight on the third Friday prior to Stoat Tuesday, and you use a real Viking bow and arrow.

Bibliographical Notes

In such stentorian historical tomes as this, it's traditional to name the sources and books from which the author culled (or pinched) the information. So here goes -

As well as reading Sir Francis Drake's book "*Eboracum*", written in 1736, well after his victory over The Spanish Armada, I have also ploughed my way through G Benson's "*An Account of the City and County of York from the Reformation to the Year 1925*"

Others are listed as follows -

A Monk; "*The Lindisfarne Gospels, Painting By Numbers.*"
Snorri Snorrison; "*A Thousand and One Viking Sagas.*"
William T. Conqueror "*The Domesday Book - A Warning!*"
St. John of the Black Bagge; "*Dafte English Folk Customs.*"
O. Cromwell; "*New Model Army; A Discography.*"
Daniel Defoe; "*A Guide to York's Fast Food Stalls.*"
Lucky Jim's Big Book of Merrie England.
The I Spy Book Of Medieval Warts and Other Nasty Things
Rev. W. Audley; "*Thomas The Tank Engine Visits York.*"
The Observer's Book of York Pavements
Tony Mallett; "*York Pubs I Have (been) Drunk In.*"
Miles Wormwood; "*York - Phew What a City!*"
Silas Shinkicker; "*York City - Phew What a Team!*"
Bill Gates; "*Microsoft Word for the Clinically Insane.*"

And finally -
"*Tinkie Winkie, Dipsey, La La & Po's Bumper Joke Book.*"

The Author.

Graham Rhodes is a writer living near York. His age is a trade secret, but he's old enough to remember the 60's and still plays music by Country Joe and The Fish. Amongst his many jobs are design work for The Police, The Cramps, Squeeze and many other bands of the late 70's. He has also been a communications designer, creating and producing audio visual presentations, conferences and videos.

As well as writing scripts for use in corporate, training and marketing videos, he has also written many historical scripts for use in museums, visitor centres and television documentaries.

Graham also writes a unique brand of stand-up comedy poetry which he performs in rock venues throughout Britain.

He smokes too much, drinks too many cups of coffee in a day, and, whenever he can afford it, tries to drink to excess. This is his fourth book (God help us!)

His Other Books Are -

York's Visible History
Leeds' Visible History
More Poems About Sex'n Drugs'n Rock'n Roll.